Getting Things Done

Stories of Leadership
from the South Bend Mayor's Office
to the School Board,
the Peace Corps and Beyond

Roger Parent
Mayor of South Bend, Indiana 1980-1987

◆　　◆　　◆

Getting Things Done

Stories of Leadership
from the South Bend Mayor's Office
to the School Board,
the Peace Corps and Beyond

Published by:
Filibuster Press, LLC
818 East Maxwell Lane, Bloomington, Indiana 47401

———

SBN: 978-0-9644007-3-3

For Orders and Information Please Contact
Filibuster Press, LLC
www.filibusterpress.com

or contact
Roger O. Parent
Email: rogerop@gmail.com
www.rogerparent.org

———

Book and Cover Design: Donald Nelson
Editor: John Monczunski

Printed in the United States of America

This Book is Dedicated to

City Employees
Whose commitment to service and hard work
make South Bend a great place to live and work.

———•———

Also to my wife Rolande, whose unstinting support
made my work and this book possible, and to
my children, Melissa, Noel, Denise and Michelle, and
my grandchildren,
Benjamin, Annika, Collin, Jacob, Gianna, Ciara

Contents

Chapter 8 Who Polluted the Water and More

Chapter 9 What I Learned on the School Board

Chapter 10 Getting Things Done in the Peace Corps

Chapter 11 Creating World Dignity, Inc.

Chapter 12 Reflections on Democracy and Politics

Appendix: Additional Acknowledgments

Acknowledgements

No Man is an Island. I have many people to thank and appreciate, most of all Rolande Parent, my wife of almost 60 years, without whom my life would be much less. She has made me a better person. My children, Michelle, Denise, Noel and Melissa, and their families, who have enriched my life in more ways than I can say.

My parents, Noel and Blanche (Corbin) Parent were the first to teach me about the importance of community in our small Acadian French village of Lille, Maine. From them I learned the value of hard work and the importance of education. I owe what I've accomplished to Rolande, my parents and my children.

Following college and two years as a Peace Corps Volunteer in Thailand, I arrived in South Bend to study at Notre Dame, and quickly came to appreciate the dynamism and resiliency of this community. I adopted it as my own and South Bend adopted me too. They elected me to the city council, mayor, and the school board. I thank the people of South Bend for the opportunity to serve and the volunteers who worked hard to get me elected.

Many citizens have given me credit for accomplishments during my time in office. (Note to current and future public servants: many accolades came long after I left office.) Citizens tend to appreciate bricks and mortar projects such as the Coveleski Stadium (now Four Winds Field), the kayak course, the ethanol plant, and neighborhood projects. I understand that.

More important than the physical projects was the highly qualified staff that brought the bricks and mortar projects to reality. They did the hard work with the required tenacity to get them done. Objective observers of the city administration noted at the time that I had the most competent staff of any city. I agreed. Without them, nothing much would have happened.

This book is the product of many people whose advice was invaluable. Readers include: Jack Colwell, South Bend Tribune Columnist; Kyle Hannon, Filibuster Press publisher; Craig E. Hartzer, associate faculty member, O'Neill School of Public and Environmental Affairs, IUPUI; Jim Lopach, professor emeritus, Political Science, University of Montana; Jean Luckowski, professor Emeritus, Education, University of Montana; John Monczunski, retired associate editor, Notre Dame Magazine; William Murphy, Executive Director, RIPEA; Don Nelson, retired art director, Notre Dame Magazine; William Odell, Outreach coordinator, Little Flower Catholic Church; Rolande Parent, my spouse; Noel Parent, my son; Richard J. Pfeil, Pfeil Inc.; St. Joseph County Council; Philip Schatz, Erasmus Book Store owner; Luther Taylor, retired South Bend Fire Chief; Robert Urbanski, retired business executive.

———

SPECIAL THANKS

TO

ROBERT J. AND DEBBIE URBANSKI

FOR THEIR GENEROUS SUPPORT

OF POLITICS THAT GETS THING DONE

AND FOR ALL THE HELP THEY PROVIDE

TO MANY COMMUNITY PROJECTS

———

Preface

Mayor Pete drew national attention to South Bend, even international attention. Journalists came from across the oceans for stories about Mayor Pete Buttigieg, about his spectacular rise in presidential polls and what he accomplished as mayor.

During his two terms, there were impressive accomplishments: A booming downtown. Impressive condo and apartment developments. New and expanded businesses. A halt in population decline.

Visiting journalists would ask if Buttigieg really did all that. And I'd say "no, not by himself." But I stressed quickly that he deserved credit as the catalyst, for the leadership in developing a "can do" civic spirit to replace finally the "can't do" influence of naysayers in the doldrums for decades after demise of Studebaker automotive production.

But Mayor Pete didn't do it all by himself, and never claimed that he did. He seized the moment for the city's future and built on its resilience in the past.

If there had not been a foundation on which to build, who would have built?

Mayor Roger Parent, who also served two terms, 1980-1987, was a leader in building that foundation, often overcoming those naysayers who insisted that South Bend just couldn't afford and shouldn't try to do such things as build a baseball stadium or develop a world class whitewater kayak course downtown along the East Race of the river.

If there was no baseball stadium, would there have been all the impressive development in the area around it and civic enthusiasm for the South Bend Cubs?

If the site of the whitewater kayak course had remained an old dumping ground, would there have been

4

all those developments along the river, the businesses, the apartments, the condos?

If Mayor Parent had not built that foundation, with other important developments as well, would Mayor Buttigieg have been able to deliver all that he did as a rising economy provided the opportunity?

Other past mayors also helped to keep the Rust Belt city from rusting away so much that Buttigieg would have had little chance to bring it back for favorable national and international attention.

Parent now writes about those critical times when South Bend built a stronger foundation.

He tells in this book about the resurrection of the baseball stadium, seemingly killed so often by those naysayers.

He discloses a key meeting with a Republican governor to save the stadium. It was agreed by the participants that officially the meeting "never happened." But it did. And he can tell about it now.

He expresses views on government and politics that differ sharply from those of the combatants in the partisan wars today. The Democratic mayor worked with Republican officials, especially with a helpful governor and senator, for vital projects for the city.

He describes also his other efforts as a city councilman, on the school board, in the Peace Corps and with founding of "World Dignity," a nonprofit corporation with focus on helping students in economically poor regions abroad.

There are admissions of mistakes, accounts with humor about such dramas as a python on the loose and some advice for political officeholders and for those who choose them. Most of all, there is the story of a foundation that prevented South Bend from ever really being a dying city.

— *Jack Colwell, South Bend Tribune Columnist*

5

Introduction

This book has been a lifetime in the making, but in its writing, not so long. After leaving the South Bend mayor position at the end of 1987, I left to direct the Peace Corps in Haiti where chaos caused by military coups had forced the evacuation of the volunteers. I had time on my hands, so I outlined issues and stories of my years as mayor and city councilman. My intent was to show how elected officials and those interested in public service can get things done in the public arena. But the volunteers returned and I put my notes away.

The theme of this book, getting things done, stems from what I learned from my father, a master carpenter. His way was to get started on a big project without worrying how it would get done and then get it done. My dad's way followed me to St. Francis Xavier University in Nova Scotia where I received a bachelor's degree in economics, magna cum laude, and to Thailand as a volunteer in the first Peace Corps group. I got things done there, even being asked to mentor other volunteers.

After Thailand, I married Rolande Ouellette, a farmer's daughter who really knows how to get things done, and arrived in South Bend to study at the University of Notre Dame where I earned a master's degree in education. Running out of money to support my growing family (eventually four children and six grandchildren) I was hired to direct South Bend's four anti-poverty program neighborhood centers. There I learned much about poverty in South

Bend and its varied ethnic and racial groups.

Wanting to do more for my community, I ran for the city council where I served for eight years, five as its president. Then I ran for mayor to get more done for South Bend. After eight years as mayor and more than 20 years in politics, I decided to leave the work I had begun for others to continue. Which led me to Haiti.

After Haiti, I served in a variety of positions and established with Rolande and a few friends, World Dignity, Inc. which operates educational programs in Thailand, South India and Bangladesh. In addition to programs in schools, we focus on supporting economically poor students in university. Currently, we have over 25 students in college and about 60 who have graduated.

Meanwhile I ran for the school board and was elected, serving more than five years, working hard with not enough success to get things done for our students. I also served as an adjunct instructor at Indiana University South Bend and Purdue / IU in Indianapolis for a few years. Along the way, I wrote and published a memoir, *The Making of a Peace Corps Volunteer: From Maine to Thailand*, and wrote magazine articles about life in Lille, an Acadian French-speaking village in northern Maine, and wrote an unpublished novel, *Amelia Discovers the Secret of Her Dove*.

About five years ago, I picked up my decades-old notes written in Haiti and wrote this book.

Chapter 1 Beginning

My Brief and Personal Take on South Bend

My wife Rolande and I arrived in South Bend in our "Unsafe at Any Speed" Chevy Corvair from Los Angeles, California, in late 1964 for graduate studies at Notre Dame. We had shipped the car from Hilo, Hawaii, where I had been training volunteers for Peace Corps service.

We didn't know much about Notre Dame and even less about South Bend. We needed to buy food, so we drove south on Michigan Street until we found a grocery store open that Sunday afternoon. On the way we were impressed by the large Robertson's Department Store and the big Sears a few blocks off Michigan. We had lived nowhere but in a small Maine village (plus Thailand village for me) and small Hilo. We were pleased to be in a city with a thriving downtown.

We had arrived at a challenging time for South Bend – the Studebaker Corporation had announced in late 1963 its decision to leave South Bend – but we did not think South Bend was a dying city. Nor have we ever thought so during decades here.

It's easy but wrong for the news media and politicians to superficially characterize South Bend as dying because of population loss. To do so does not factor in South Bend's underlying strengths, and it's misleading.

The news media hype ignores the vitality of South Bend's major institutions, all of which are in South Bend to stay. The city is a regional destination for culture, entertainment, museums, conventions, and sports. Its downtown includes a thriving minor league baseball stadium, a one-of-a-kind whitewater kayak course, and Notre Dame offers a wide variety of college sports events. Medical services are provided to a wide area from here, and it is the county seat with a concentration of criminal justice agencies. Increasingly, downtown is a growing market for middle and high-end apartments.

Equally significant, major institutions of higher learning are based here: Indiana University-South Bend, Saint Mary's College, University of Notre Dame, Bethel University, Ivy Tech, and Holy Cross College. These institutions are essential elements of a thriving city, and they're not moving anywhere.

There are many reasons for a community to lose population; it's not just a matter of fewer jobs. Families have gotten smaller and people have moved to the suburbs. Plus, South Bend has been specifically hampered by the state legislature from annexing suburbs, thus preventing it from expanding its population base as most cities in Indiana and elsewhere have done. In this context, it's significant to note that St. Joseph County, in which South Bend is located, has had a population increase of about 12 percent since 1960. It's fair to assume that a portion of that increase would have occurred in South Bend.

Upon arriving here in 1964, we were immediately impressed with the political, governmental, civic, and business leadership aggressively tackling the loss of jobs, a weakened tax base, and a somewhat disheartened citizenry. One community leader led the way by famously saying: "This is not Studebaker, Indiana. This is South Bend, Indiana." South Bend and the region have been well served by strong leadership since the early days of deindustrialization, globalization, and job loss.

Rolande and I chose South Bend as our home because of the vitality of its major institutions, its energetic leadership, and the strength and diversity of its people. South Bend is well-positioned for a bright future and we're happy to continue being a part of it.

*****

South Bend is located in north central Indiana about 100 miles east of Chicago. It was established as a town in 1835 and incorporated as a city in 1865, although it was born much earlier. The Potawatomi tribe occupied the area until the majority was forcibly removed in the 1840s.

The first non-native permanent residents of South Bend were fur traders. Later a large surge of immigrants from Poland, Italy, Hungary and many other countries came to work in the burgeoning manufacturing plants of the late 19th and early 20th centuries. After the Second World War, many African Americans moved to South Bend from the South for jobs and cultural / educational opportunities. Today about 25 percent of South Bend's population is African American and about 20 percent is Hispanic and people of other national origin or races.

Who Am I?

If someone had asked me, "Who are you?" when I was
15, I wouldn't have known what to say. I might have said
something like, I'm the son of a carpenter and teacher, or
I'm Acadian French who lives in a village in Maine. Today, I
barely recognize the 15 year-old kid who thought he would
live in his village forever. I'm older now and the question is
harder. Family, community, culture, books, teachers, friends,
colleagues, and time have influenced and changed my view
on life.

It was not the norm in the 1950s that the children of
a carpenter in rural Maine would go to college, but my parents thought we should get more schooling, not so much for
a better job, but for more knowledge. Learning was important
in my home. I attended St. Francis Xavier University in Nova
Scotia, participated in campus politics, and received a bachelor's degree in economics and politics in 1961.

1961 was lucky for me. That was the year President
John F. Kennedy took office and said he would establish the

Peace Corps. "Ask not what your country can do for you – ask what you can do for your country," he said. I was inspired, but had no inspired plan. All I knew was that I wanted to help people and have an adventure.

So even before the Peace Corps was formed, I wrote to President Kennedy and volunteered my services. In short order, I was asked to take a battery of tests, was accepted for Thailand, trained at the University of Michigan, and arrived in Bangkok on January 22, 1962, my 23rd birthday – a perfect gift.

Thailand was more than a birthday gift, it was the gift of acquiring a new language, learning about Buddhism, and being immersed in a new culture. My way of seeing the world was being altered, sometimes in dramatic fashion.

At a horrendous bus accident, (I was on the bus) I was conflicted by my Catholic teaching that the dying cyclist who had been run over could not enter heaven unless he were baptized. I thought about baptizing him, but my newly acquired respect for the generosity of Buddhists told me that good people, no matter their religion, would go to heaven.

When my Thai colleagues said, "We can make babies but cannot make trucks and trains," to explain why they were not overly concerned about the lives lost in a truck-train collision (as I was), I learned how scarce resources can trump human life.

After two years of learning and growing in Thailand, I returned to marry Rolande in Maine (1963), attended the University of Notre Dame in Indiana where I received a master's degree in education (1966), and continued for a doctorate. I left the doctoral program after I ran out of money to support my growing family. I needed a job.

In 1967, just four years after the Studebaker Corporation had shut down, jobs were scarce in South Bend, but I was fortunate to get a job in the anti-poverty program. There I came face to face with urban poverty, culture, and racial discrimination. This was entirely different from my experience of rural Maine poverty and culture as a child, and from my experience of Thailand poverty and culture as a young adult.

Growing up in the rural Maine Acadian-French-speaking culture, acquiring carpentry skills from my father, learning from books and other students at Saint Francis Xavier University, maturing in Thailand's Buddhist culture, being married with children, and being immersed in the problems of urban poverty through my work were experiences I brought to South Bend politics and government in 1972.

My Father Said, "Stop Thinking and Take the First Step"

One day while walking around with my father trying to figure out the best orientation of a house on a hilly, stony lot, he said, "If we're going to build this house we better start."

From my carpenter father, I learned to hit a nail on the head, to saw a board in a straight line, and to visualize a house from a hole in the ground. But the most enduring, maybe the most practical lesson I learned from him was that taking the first step, not quite knowing the next, was the way to tackle any project, big or small, simple or complicated.

I didn't realize it then, but reflecting on my life now, I know how important that lesson was to me. It translated not only to physical projects but to major life and career decisions. I learned to take the first step without worrying much, if at all, about what would come next and how to handle whatever happened. I made major life decisions and took on major projects without knowing fully how I would see them through.

I volunteered for the Peace Corps in 1961 before it

was established. I didn't know what it would be like, nor did I have any idea what being a Peace Corps Volunteer would involve. Much later, in 1971, when I took my first step into politics and filed for Fourth District councilman, I had no knowledge of how to run a political campaign or how to be a city councilman. And when I ran for mayor, I knew a bit more about politics, but did not fully appreciate the challenges which lay ahead in the campaign and in being an effective mayor.

When a group of citizens asked me to build a whitewater kayak course in downtown South Bend, I said yes knowing little about the funding, engineering, and construction challenges it would entail. And when a group of baseball fans asked me to build a minor league baseball stadium, I agreed and built it in downtown South Bend – said then to be the first minor league stadium in a downtown.

My father was right, taking the first step, not quite knowing the next, was the way to go. I wish he were still around to hear me say this.

Chapter 2
Learning City Politics
and Government

Would You Want
Your Child
to Go into Politics?

If you ask a mother or father, "would you want your children to run for political office?" most would say no. People generally think that politics is a crooked business, that to be a politician, you either have to be a crook, or become one to be successful.

My parents never voiced an opinion about what career I should pursue. However, when I was 30 years old and told them I had decided to run for the city council, they cautioned me to be honest at all times. And when, as a teenager, I had mentioned to my pastor I was interested in going into politics, he warned me not to do so, "Too many politicians are dishonest," he said. Ironically, politicians themselves often reflect this thinking by saying, "Vote for me, I'm not a politician."

Politics is a high calling in a grubby world. Politicians must and do compromise to establish workable laws and policies for a wide variety of people. Compromise is part of politics because we live in an imperfect world. As James Madison said, laws and policies are made for imperfect men and women, not for angels. Politicians who deal with these imperfections are often seen as mirroring those imperfections.

Politics is more demanding intellectually, emotionally,

physically, and morally than most people fully understand. Only people with strong convictions and principles who are not in it to be loved – the occupational hazard of being a politician – should seek political office. To be elected, you seek approval, even to be loved, yet to govern, you inevitably make decisions that will disappoint people.

So, you may ask, why did I run for the city council, then mayor, then the school board? The most honest answer is that I don't quite know. When people ask me why I joined the Peace Corps in 1961, I tell them I wanted to help poor people in a poor country. But now I know I also wanted adventure, and maybe something else I'm not aware of today. When I ran for the city council in 1971, I told people I wanted to help create a better community, but I'm sure there was more to it than that.

Today, decades later, I think my political involvement reflected deep-seated tendencies which emanated from the lives and decisions of my parents, grandparents, and other ancestors. But I didn't appreciate that in my younger life, I thought I was making rational decisions about a career that interested me.

How to Campaign for Councilman

I didn't know anything about being a candidate for a political office nor how to run a political campaign. I didn't know much about the job of city councilman – councilmember was not even the first position I had considered – I wanted to be Mayor of South Bend, but my friends and acquaintances fast disabused me of that notion. They said I'd make a fine mayor, but I couldn't win. Reluctantly, I agreed, and as they suggested, I ran for Fourth District councilman.

My interest in politics had been stimulated by my older brother, Paul, who had been impressed with then candidate for President John F. Kennedy. My first vote was for Kennedy – I had been excited by his idea for the Peace Corps which I joined in 1961. And while at St. Francis Xavier University in Nova Scotia, I had helped in the campus mock campaign of the New Party which had won.

The question was how to be a candidate and how to run a political campaign. Having somewhat of an academic bent, (I'd spent three years in graduate school at Notre

Dame), I decided to hit the books. I spent time in the local library and in those of Notre Dame and Indiana University-South Bend. I found many books on political theory and many political memoirs, but little on how to organize and run a political campaign. What to do? If I couldn't get how-to-knowledge from books, I would go to the people of politics – local elected officials and people deeply involved in politics. They would know how to run a campaign. I didn't know them and wondered if they'd want to meet with me.

I called the county and district Democratic Party chairs and many prominent Democrats. I said I was running for Fourth District councilman, asked to meet them for their advice and to consider supporting me. In the late 60s and early 70s it had been traditional to ask the party elders for permission to run. I didn't do that because I thought that was a weak position to take.

They were not miffed at this, and seemed eager, maybe even flattered, to be asked for advice. They emphasized there was a long-time party person seeking the Fourth District post and that it would be hard for me to win. However, they did not discourage me from running.

They told me to keep talking with Democratic Party leaders and gave me names of other people to call, giving me permission to use their names when calling them. I was not getting their blessings, but they were being very helpful. They told me to go door-to-door, attend political rallies, put up many yard signs and recruit volunteers to be at the polls on election day to greet voters. The latter, they said, was when most voters decided on lower races such as for the city council, unfortunately.

My seeking advice and support from party activists and officials was the best way I could have approached the task of running. The word got out among Democrats and the community of voters generally, that this "young kid" was working hard and had a future in Democratic politics – not that I would win this time, but could do so later. They were eager to have me continue in local Democratic politics.

It worked. I easily won the Democratic nomination and the general election. I had worked very hard, visited almost every home in the district, delivered brochures, installed hundreds of yard signs, and had met citizens in neighborhood coffees. What I learned in this first campaign gave me the experience to successfully run many more for councilman, mayor and the school board.

I became known for my grassroots-type campaigns. Today, people come to me for advice on how to run political campaigns. It's my turn.

Free Notre Dame
Football Tickets and
Free Movies

Soon after I was elected to the to the South Bend City Council in November 1971, the University of Notre Dame sent me free football game tickets and I got free movie passes from local theatres.

I was new to politics, but not so naïve to miss the reason for the gifts; those were intended for special access, or favors, at the expense of the citizenry. I was dismayed at their assumption about me, but not surprised. Such practices to establish friendly relationships with elected officials were waning in South Bend, but still prevalent. Businesses and individuals were simply doing what they had always done to curry favor with elected officials. Anyway, they did not have to give me gifts to have access. I would have met with anyone who had a serious (and some not so serious) matter to discuss.

I immediately returned those gifts with a letter stating: "It's my policy as an elected official to not accept any gifts / remuneration other than my openly approved council member salary." The letter was released to the media to let the public know of my position on the matter of gifts to me.

The University of Notre Dame and the movie houses

did not object, and I don't remember receiving another gift from them during my 21 years in elected office. Later, I learned that some, maybe all local elected officials, stopped receiving these gifts too. They blamed me for losing those free-bees. The attitude seemed to be, "who do you think you are coming here and upsetting the gravy train? We deserve this for all the work we do for the city which pays us very little."

Eight years later, when elected mayor in 1979, remnants of this pay-for-favors practice came to my attention. I was approached by a few persons who asked me, "how much will I have to pay you to get my son appointed to the fire or police departments?" It had not been long past that individuals might have to give – I was told $500 – to the mayor's bagman to be appointed a firefighter or police officer . . . maybe for other city jobs too. My response to those persons was, "if you approach me again with this question, I will refer the matter to the prosecutor's office." The word soon got around and I was not approached this way after my first months in office.

Notwithstanding these experiences as councilman (1972 – 1979), mayor (1980 – 1987), and school board member (2009 – 2014), politics in South Bend has been generally clean for decades. On the whole, honesty with money is not a large problem with local elected officials, honesty with words is the much more serious challenge to our democracy.

Can a Politician Convince Citizens He/She Is Not a Crook?

Other than breaking a few windows in a long-abandoned house in my rural Maine village, I'm not aware of laws I may have broken. Oh, maybe a few speeding tickets. When I decided to go into politics, I was cautioned by my father about the difficulty of being an honest politician. "Stay honest," he said.

Most politicians are honest with money, if not with words. Nevertheless, many persons believe that most, if not all politicians, are on the take. True, there are crooked politicians, and when they're caught, their faces are plastered for days on newspapers, television and social media. On the other hand, if a top-tiered white collar worker is discovered with his hands in the till, it's often handled quietly out of the public eye. Thus, a politician, even one new to politics, is often assumed to be dishonest.

What's a politician to do? The late President Richard Nixon tried by telling the public, "I am not a crook." It didn't work and he resigned before being impeached. Sometimes a dishonest politician can convince a majority of the public he

25

or she is honest. But thankfully, this doesn't always work. I believe, as Abraham Lincoln said in 1856, that "Actions speak louder than words."

So, in 1971 during my first campaign for the South Bend City Council, I published a detailed personal financial statement, a practice I continued during my campaigns for elected office. A councilman said at the time, half-jokingly, "No wonder you published your finances, you're not worth much of anything." We laughed. But maybe there was some truth in his comment. What if I had been worth millions, would I have published my finances? I like to think I would have.

My published financial statement was given wide coverage in the local media. There was no law that required filing a personal financial statement of any kind, let alone a detailed one. I did so to let the public know I was not seeking public office to benefit financially other than to accept the publicly approved salary for the position.

In spite of releasing public personal financial statements, there were people who accused me, often to my face, of benefiting illegally from some of my public actions. Once, in a popular restaurant where I was dining with a reporter, a well-dressed man came up to me and asked how much money I had been paid to build a baseball stadium in South Bend. My quick question to him was, "Are you asking me that because that's what you would have done in my place?" He didn't say anything. Later he came back to apologize, but few people were gracious enough to do so.

Another time, a person wrote to me that I had accepted a "commission" to get a major building in downtown South Bend demolished. In this case, I called him and also wrote him a detailed letter, telling him he was wrong, that I had not accepted a "commission" as he had accused me. He didn't apologize.

On the whole, my public and private comments about

not accepting gifts and publishing my personal financial statements did get through sufficiently to the community. Jack Colwell, South Bend Tribune reporter and columnist, wrote in an end-of-my-final term article, "He was a pioneer around here in release of personal finance statements. He steered clear of conflicts of interest . . ."

I Was Determined to Pay a 50-Year-Old City Debt Owed its Citizens.

I was shocked to learn early in my first term as mayor in 1980 that the city owed its citizens a debt dating to the 1930s. Citizens had bought South Bend, Indiana Improvement Bonds during the 1930s Depression and bond holders had not been fully paid.

I immediately asked the city's legal department to research the legal issues and old record books about paying the bond holders. I didn't see this old debt as junk, something to be left in the ashcan of history. I saw it as a commitment, indeed, a responsibility of the city, just as I saw a personal debt as a responsibility. I was determined to pay this old debt.

In 1940, bondholders had sued the city after it had failed to fully meet its obligations and the court had ordered the city to issue a $1.65 million bond to cover its debt. But when some bond holders got dissatisfied with the manner in which the city was paying off the bonds, the city was sued again. The judge had frozen the dedicated fund pending a thorough review of the situation, and then he had died. The fund had remained frozen since his death.

It turned out to be a long story that took a few years

to unravel. Finally, in early 1984, after the legal work and other requirements were completed, the fund was "thawed" and paying the bonds could begin. The city advertised in the South Bend Tribune and the Midwest edition of the Wall Street Journal stating that South Bend was prepared to redeem those old bonds and retire the debt. The account had grown from $249,656.57 to $782,493.42 due to interest earned on the principal.

Few people remembered the debt prior to the advertisements and news accounts, and those who still held bond certificates had likely seen them as junk. Citizens were impressed that some people during the Depression had been so civic minded as to invest in their city, and they were also impressed that I would go to great lengths, almost 50 years later, to pay this ancient debt.

The bonds were not junk to the 81 persons whose claims were paid. One person was paid $34,760.64. A bank that held bonds in trust got $25,708.45. Most claims were for less than $1,000.

One claimant said, "I'm grateful that someone took the time to look into this and to make good on the debt. They probably could have let it go." Another claimant said she kept the bonds because they were very elaborate and interesting. She gushed, "Yesterday I had nothing, and today I've got this." In the end the city received around $400,000 left over from unredeemed bonds.

My view of this old city debt probably came from my father's way of thinking: You pay a debt because it's a sacred responsibility. During the Depression a neighbor had loaned him money he hadn't asked for to build his house. She trusted him more than she trusted the banks.

I felt the way my father did about South Bend's debt to its citizens. I had not decided to pay this debt to enhance the city's already strong credit rating, but to send a strong message that South Bend's promises are as good as gold.

My First Day as Mayor: Disappointment

My first day as mayor, my first department directors' meeting, and what do I have to cope with? A racist joke. People were milling around waiting for the meeting to start when I overheard a director making a racist joke. I can't say I was shocked. I'd heard racist jokes before, but I was disappointed in this person. I was also disappointed in myself. Hadn't we vetted him adequately?

As we were waiting for latecomers – something which aggravated me but would deal with later – I wondered how to handle those racist words. I had not expected that kind of talk, especially by a top administrator, and I was not going to tolerate it. Indeed, by temperament I could not tolerate it.

Most people don't know this, but being Acadian French (or any French) in Maine meant being discriminated against by English speakers since Maine's beginnings. This discrimination was embedded in my flesh and bones. My 1960s work in South Bend's antipoverty program had strengthened what I'd learned. Beneath our skins and below the surface of our cultures, we are all the same and deserve to be treated equally with dignity and respect.

I was new to the mayor's job, but I was sure it was my responsibility to set high standards and expectations for all city workers. So I began the meeting with a discussion of the racist joke. I had not intended to start my first staff meeting on what could be seen as a negative note, but it was called for by the joke. Maybe it was the gift of a teachable moment. It was certainly a learning moment for me.

I didn't see myself as better than anyone else. I had learned early to respect every person regardless of their views. The person who had made the comment was likely raised in a home and hung around with friends who did not realize how hurtful this kind of talk is.

I told the staff about the joke without naming the person who had made it and said I didn't appreciate that kind of talk in the workplace, or anywhere else. "I can't stop anyone from having those thoughts, but I expect everyone to treat all city workers and citizens with dignity and respect. You don't have to like the people you work with, although it makes work more fun and productive if you do."

I was determined to immediately set a different tone and atmosphere for the work place. In a small way I did. No other racist joke or comment was made in my presence during my eight years as mayor.

If the Barn is Red,
Paint It Green

"If the barn is red, paint it green." That's what Clifford MacMillan (Mac) told me. "You're the new kid on the block," he said, "you have to take early dramatic action to establish that your administration and leadership will be different."

I was mayor-elect and Mac had volunteered his services to advise me on general management matters and to help select top quality staff. He had been Studebaker Corporation Vice-President of Industrial Relations for decades until Studebaker closed its South Bend operations in 1963.

Mac was wise in the ways of management, bureaucracies, and employee relations. I valued his advice, but more important to me, we became friends. He had a terrific sense of humor which helped me navigate difficult and sometimes tense situations. Whenever a failing business acquires another failing business, I think of his vivid description of the 1950s Studebaker-Packard merger as "Two drunks trying to help each other across the street."

Mac was concerned that my low key leadership style could be misinterpreted as weak and lacking the nerve to take the strong and courageous actions needed to build a strong administration. He emphasized the necessity of sending an unequivocal message that I was firmly committed to building a professional work force totally dedicated to serving the public, and that I would not tolerate anything less. He repeated, "You have to take early visible action to communicate your leadership style."

It didn't take long for an opportunity to come up – before I was sworn in as mayor. A mid-level supervisor in the Water Works Bureau was notorious for "drinking his lunch" and dozing off in the afternoon. He was the brother of a local popular judge and he boasted often he'd never be fired because of his brother's political clout. History had proven him right: no former mayor or administrator had fired or demoted him.

I knew this employee well. He had supported another person in the Democratic primary and now he was going around the city wearing a cap which read, "Dump Parent," boasting his job was secure. To be clear, I would not terminate him or anyone else for supporting another candidate. That's not my way. I didn't fire people for political reasons. Anyway, in this case, I had a legitimate reason to take action.

Here was my opportunity to send a strong message to the work force, their friends and supporters. I decided to let him know that come January 1 when I would take office, he would not have a job with the city. My administrative assistant-to-be delivered the news to him prior to my swearing-in ceremony. His reaction was that his brother would call me and protect his job. Political operatives said I'd made a serious political mistake which would jeopardize my ambitious agenda for the city.

As it turned out, I didn't hear from the judge. This highly professional and dedicated judge understood my motivation and did not intervene. He never called me and we remained on friendly terms. Even if he had called, I wouldn't have changed my mind. Once I've made a considered decision, I stick with it no matter the political cost.

Actually, the reaction by many was that it was about time someone did something about this employee.

Are You Getting Too Big for Your Britches, Mr. Mayor?

A citizen scolded me for not noticing him while I was walking to a meeting, "Who do you think you are?" he asked. "I said 'hi' to you and you didn't respond." I had been totally preoccupied with an issue that was probably not even important, but when concentrating on something, I tend not to hear or even be aware of the people around me. It took me a while to reconcile the view that although I didn't think being mayor made me more important as a person, the position was important and it was a big deal to citizens. To me being mayor was a job to do and doing it well was the big deal.

I had served on the city council for eight years, had been council president five of those years, and after a tough campaign, I'd become mayor. I was eager to take on the challenge of leading South Bend for four years. The people had voted convincingly for a different leadership and I was determined to provide it. Changes had to be made in the top management of most departments and I had to do so quickly in time for swearing-in on January 1. I wanted to hit the ground running.

Everything was moving on schedule until I set out to make changes in the top administrators of the fire department, when the City Attorney-to-be said, "Roger you can demote the fire chief for any reason, but you cannot demote assistant chiefs except for cause, which they can appeal. State law has changed and mayors are not allowed to demote those ranks for political reasons or just because you want assistant chiefs more amenable to your management style."

Over the years, I had seen mayors make changes in the top ranks of the fire department, demoting top personnel and promoting others to chief and assistant chiefs. I was prepared to do that. But the attorney insisted that I could not demote the three assistant chiefs.

"What do you mean I can't demote all these ranks?" I asked. "This has been the practice for as long as I can remember. I'm the mayor and I'm expected to provide a new kind of leadership to the city, especially in the fire department, and you're telling me I cannot make those changes in personnel."

"Roger, I'm sorry but that's the situation according to state law."

I'm quite sure I pushed my point too far as I'm wont to do, and he probably became a bit exasperated with me. Although I know he felt that being mayor was a big deal, he knew I had to follow the statute. He didn't say that if I didn't take his advice, I should look for another person to be City Attorney, but he might have felt like doing so.

I was frustrated. It seemed to me that I couldn't appoint the personnel needed to provide the high quality services I had promised and citizens expected. Nevertheless, I reluctantly followed his advice. Good thing I did. The mayor of another Indiana city did what I had wanted to do, was sued, lost in court and her city had to pay large sums to the fire fighters and police officers demoted.

Ultimately, the strong principled people I'd selected for top posts, who were willing to question any authority, especially mine, made me the kind of mayor I wanted to be – one who didn't get a chance to get too big for his britches.

What? Me Wishy-Washy?
Me Pigheaded?

When I was city councilman, some people called me wishy-washy and when I was mayor some people – maybe the same people – called me pigheaded. I didn't like those names and certainly didn't see myself as wishy-washy or pigheaded. Anyway, as councilman, I didn't fret over being seen as wishy-washy, but as mayor I wanted to better understand how people could see me in such diametrically opposite ways. I could have ignored those names, but I knew those skewed perceptions could hinder my work as mayor.

I'm no psychologist, but a small amount of introspection (politicians are not so inclined nor have much time to introspect) led me to understand better my different roles as councilman and as mayor. The two positions demanded different approaches and skills which likely highlighted different aspects of my makeup.

Leadership by a member of any legislative body involves convincing other members of one's position. True, a mayor has a similar task, but does so from a different angle that carries more weight. Very often, taking an early definitive public stand on an issue doesn't help to modify, adopt, or defeat an issue. I was more focused on directly changing the minds of council members than on influencing the general public to pressure them. I thought that could be done more easily in private conversations.

It could be that my approach came in part from my desire to nurture my relationships with council members to attain the presidency of the council. Maybe not. Anyway, having good working relationships with colleagues on a legislative body is a plus no matter the underlying motives.

Early in my first term on the city council, the mayor proposed around $300,000 for an existing small drug rehabilitation center in the northeast neighborhood that I represented. The center had become somewhat controversial, in part because it was in the middle of a residential area. Some people living close by opposed it; others living a bit further from the facility were for it. I supported it too. Some council members were opposed to the proposal because they thought it was an inappropriate use of municipal funds, others felt the facility should not be in a residential area, and some probably just didn't like the mayor.

The mayor wanted me to take a strong public position on the issue prior to the council meeting. I resisted. I thought it would be best to talk privately and quietly with individual council members to secure their support for it.

After a council meeting, four or five of us would go for a beer or two and greasy food at a councilman's bar on Portage avenue to unwind. We enjoyed being together after council meetings and often reached a meeting of minds on issues without fully realizing it. A councilman who had opposed the drug rehabilitation center proposal said, "Roger, I know you're pushing that $300,000 funding and although I'm not in favor, I could go along with half that amount." Another said, "I could do that too." The elements of a compromise were coming together.

During the public hearing on the bill, I moved to amend the amount by half, it was seconded and passed. As one long-time councilmember who had opposed the mayor's proposal said, "Half a loaf is better than none."

I was pleased with the result, but quite surprised that many people were not happy with me. The mayor scolded me, "I had the votes for the full amount and you spoiled my plan."

People who opposed the center were upset that the bill did not die outright, and many of the academics in the area seemed to prefer that the whole proposal die rather than see it reduced and adopted. Maybe that approach made them feel superior to weak-spine politicians.

I was quite naïve then, as I still am on many issues. I thought citizens who supported the proposal would be satisfied to get something and those who opposed it would not be upset with the compromise. I was so wrong. I was a hero to no one, and through the compromise I had initiated, I had started down the path of being seen as wishy-washy.

That changed soon after being elected mayor when police officers decided on a "blue flu" action to force me to accept their demands during a salary negotiation. They had seen me as weak and thought such an action would force me to give in to them.

Testing the New Mayor:
Police Blue Flu

"The blue flu has begun. They're calling in sick with the flu said the police chief. This was Saturday around midnight of Memorial Day weekend, 1980. I was at the city controller's house partying after a long week's work. "We'll be at the police station in 15 minutes." And so we were – the adrenaline surging against the alcohol we had consumed.

Not long after I was sworn in as mayor, January 1, 1980, rumors had quickly surfaced that police officers were going to come down with a blue flu – typically, a case of police officers falsely calling in sick to support their union's contract demands. Negotiations with the city council had stalled. Still, this didn't make much sense as a union tactic since contract talks had not yet matured to that critical stage. I believed it was more about testing me, perceived by many police officers as weak, or as they put it, wishy-washy.

The City Attorney and I had decided early that if we were going to be tested, we were going to be ready for it. The

41

City Attorney, who had primary responsibility for overseeing the police department, had created a team and developed a plan for the rumored "flu." It included the city controller (Vietnam POW), the public safety director (a tough-as-nails Vietnam War helicopter pilot), and a skilled assistant attorney who later became the city's first woman City Attorney.

We immediately put in action the City Attorney's plan. Speed was the order of the day. The public would not have tolerated a work stoppage by the police department for very long, and a long work stoppage would have provided time for the police and their families to gain public sympathy for their cause.

The Board of Public Safety was convened in the wee hours of Sunday morning. It approved an order requiring medical proof of illness before police could return to work, and the police chief issued a "green alert" requiring all off-duty officers to be at or near their home. The Circuit Court quickly convened Sunday afternoon, issued a temporary restraining order to the walk-out, and authorized 100 city employees to be process servers.

Usually when this type of job action happened, a restraining order was served only to the leaders of the Fraternal Order of Police (FOP) and the members of the bargaining committee. We didn't do that. We wanted to avoid making martyrs of the FOP leadership and committee members. Instead we concentrated on serving papers to all other nonworking police officers, and by late Monday, about 80 percent had been served. If these officers had not returned to work after a reasonable period of time, they could have been brought to court. We were hoping to generate the feeling among the officers served that they, not their leaders, would be paying the price of the job action. Our goal was to divide the general FOP membership from the leaders and have them pressure the leadership to return to the negotiating table.

The impact on the police officers and their families

was palpable. Police officers who had sworn to uphold the law and hold citizens accountable for breaking the law were being told in a formal way they were breaking the law. If they didn't return to work, they could lose their jobs.

Meanwhile the state police had been called for assistance. The governor's office had earlier been informed of a possible blue flu in South Bend and had promised to assist. Three or four state police officers and all 16 South Bend police administrators (captains up to chief) were patrolling the city. All this helped to assure citizens that police protection was being provided, albeit at a lower level.

Luck was on our side. The weather on this Memorial Day weekend was cold and rainy, which caused cancelling or lowering the number of people at public events. During the weekend, there were few calls for police assistance, and fake calls from "ill" police officers were fairly easy to sort out.

When the National FOP attorney arrived in South Bend, it didn't take him long to assess the situation. He told the local FOP, "The city has you cornered and you should get back to the negotiating table. They have done everything legally correct to summon you to court and possibly fire you." Although we were prepared to do that, we were also prepared to negotiate with FOP representatives in a friendly spirit.

Through various backchannels we had indicated there would be no reprisals, officially or unofficially, if they returned to work soon. We also said we had carefully prepared briefs and were ready to go to court against unnamed officers. That made everyone on the force nervous.

On Wednesday, three days after the blue flu had begun, the officers returned to work. We fulfilled our promise and negotiated a salary and fringe benefit increase close to what had been discussed prior to the blue flu. No "salt was rubbed in the wound," there was no gloating, and we didn't even hint we had won. We said publicly that neither side had lost or won. We didn't have to since the community and the editorial board of the South Bend Tribune commended our administration. After all was said and done, police officers were our employees with whom we wanted to maintain a cordial working relationship.

Our response to the blue flu did more than anything else to dispel the thinking that I was wishy-washy.

Chapter 3
Build a Kayak Course Downtown?

I Was Asked to Create
a Kayak Course Downtown

Early in 1980, when I was focused on bringing an ethanol plant to South Bend, I was urged to create a whitewater kayak course in downtown.

Some people think the kayak course idea was mine. It was not, just as an ethanol plant and a minor league baseball stadium were not. My eight years as councilman had taught me the value of listening carefully to citizens, or maybe it was from my mother who had told me often, "Listen to me." I had learned early that excellent ideas come from many people and places.

The idea for a man-made whitewater kayak course came from a local organization, Michiana Watershed, Inc., in 1973, when I was a member of the city council. The group had commissioned a study that had recommended converting the long-abandoned raceway along the eastern bank of the St. Joseph River to a whitewater kayak course.

The East Raceway which had provided power for factories along the river in the 19th and early 20th centuries was now filled with construction debris, some of it toxic. At the time, a South Bend Tribune reporter had written that the area

46

had become "nothing more than a bunch of overgrown and underdeveloped lots."

Nothing happened to the kayak proposal for a long time. But the Watershed group kept it alive and in 1978, then-Mayor Peter J. Nemeth endorsed the idea which gave it traction. But well intended as he was in supporting the project, he finished his tenure as mayor in 1979, and the kayak project lay dormant.

The Watershed group persevered, and early in 1980, during my first year as mayor, they asked for a meeting to discuss their proposal for a whitewater kayak course in downtown South Bend. At the time, my staff and I were busy reorganizing the city administrative structure, looking for ways to diversify the fire and police departments, and seeking funds to build an ethanol plant. Still, I was willing to listen.

I approached the meeting with an open mind, yet skeptical the group could convince me that a whitewater kayak course would be a good use of city funds and a productive use of my time.

The Watershed group said this would be the first man-made whitewater course in the Americas and put South Bend on the map. It would double the downtown waterfront property available for residential and office construction, create an exciting park, and generate business for hotels and restaurants. They emphasized it would more than pay for itself by substantially increasing property taxes in an area reaping very little.

I was impressed by their argument and persuaded. We decided to build a whitewater kayak course in downtown South Bend, not knowing exactly how or where we were going to get funds. We'd have to find an estimated $5 million (More than $15 million in 2021 dollars) – funds we didn't have, plus state and federal government grants, an uncertain possibility.

Would citizens agree to spend money for a kayak course downtown?

Borrow Money for the Kayak Course?

We knew it would be difficult. To build the kayak course, we had to borrow the money. We were already scrambling to get citizen's signatures to borrow $5.9 million dollars (about $17 million in 2021 dollars) for police, fire and street department equipment. And we were seeking funds from various sources to make an ethanol plant a reality.

Borrowing money in Indiana was a convoluted and long process. Then, a city had to get permission from the public to approve a bond, and to get that permission, the city had to secure more signatures than the opposition. More nerve-wracking, once the city had filed its signatures, the opposition had additional time to get more signatures. I thought this was very unfair.

Typically, when a city decides to borrow through a bond, it includes many items to widen its support. So we added irrigating golf courses, purchasing an ice rink the city was renting, and renovating a recreation center, thus increasing the bond from $3.5 million for the kayak course to $5.8 million. About a million of the estimated $5 million kayak course cost would be sought through grants from state and federal agencies.

We thought these additional projects would make it easier to get more signatures than the opposition, but we were wrong. In spite of our efforts and the Michiana Watershed's well-organized signature gathering campaign, by the end of 1980, we concluded we would likely lose the battle of signatures. The additional projects had not helped, indeed they had intensified the opposition. I had to make a decision.

In January 1981, I asked the park board, which had to approve the project to reduce the bond amount by $2.3 million, effectively cutting the "extra" projects, leaving funding only for the kayak course. They were not happy and neither was I. But they agreed that the additional projects would have to wait, or else the entire bond proposal would probably be defeated. We were disappointed, but had no choice.

A few days later, we got a welcomed boost from a South Bend Tribune editorial that said the cuts were "wise," and the kayak course a good idea. Thank God, or rather the Tribune, which was very influential then. It helped to sustain us during the long, difficult road ahead.

Meanwhile we had another challenge. The $5.9 million bond to purchase equipment for fire, police and street departments was in trouble. We were losing that signature battle too. I had to either withdraw the petition or reduce the amount to borrow. This was a very difficult choice. I was deeply committed to excellent basic city services which we couldn't provide without those funds. Furthermore, absent excellent city services, citizens would be loathe to approve projects considered optional, such as a kayak course.

I reduced the equipment bond from $5.9 million to $3.2 million and pressed harder for signatures. We hadn't planned on being in the unusual situation of seeking signatures for two bonds simultaneously, but taking advantage of the kayak course opportunity had led to this situation.

We persisted. Slowly, as the public gained a better understanding of the whitewater kayak project and its potential for the community, signature gathering got easier. It also got easier for the equipment bond.

We garnered 5,289 signatures for the kayak course and filed them, knowing the opposition might get more signatures than we had. They were well organized and had worked hard, but it was time for us to get this resolved one way or the other and move on.

Unknown to me, the City Attorney and a few citizen allies supporting the kayak course had been meeting with a "splinter" group within the opposition to encourage them to support the kayak course and not file their signatures. Probably, he had not told me to avoid raising my hopes.

The City Attorney and citizens must have been very convincing because the splinter group decided to not file their signatures that would have defeated the kayak bond. I don't know if they were sincerely convinced of the value of the kayak course, or just did so to spite the other opposition group. Whatever.

The bond moved forward to the State Board of Tax Commissioners who voted yes. Also, State and federal grants in the amount of $1.1 million were approved. We were ready to build the kayak course.

This was a unique project – one of a kind – and we knew more hurdles remained. What would come next?

Delays and Construction Hurdles

It took more than two years after I was approached to build the kayak course in early 1980 to reach ground breaking on June 25, 1982. Even after the bond was approved by the citizenry in late 1981, and by the Indiana Tax Commissioners, in March 1982, a disgruntled citizen filed a suit that stopped progress, but only for a while. The city filed a counter suit which prompted the citizen to drop his suit.

Excavation and construction of the park department's most ambitious capital project in its history was unique, the first in the Americas. The engineers and construction crews were cutting their chops on this one. We kept our fingers crossed.

The first delay occurred even before construction began. Acquisition of properties in the east raceway took much more time than anticipated because some owners owned portions of the bed of the race while other owners owned the top soil. Don't ask me how this happened. Our lawyers and staff spent hours sorting out the ownership. Also, there was more toxic material to dig out than anticipated, which chewed up days and funds.

After thousands of tons of dirt and debris dumped in the race from various renewal projects, including debris from an old electric facility had been fully removed, a 1,900 foot channel was revealed and ready for the concrete construction. It was an exciting time.

By November, 1983, the whitewater course was ready to be tested. The gates were opened and water rushed through and filled the kayak course. It passed the test with flying colors. No problem. The city staff and the community began planning for a grand opening in June 1984.

The euphoria of the successful test was still in the air when all of a sudden huge concrete slabs were lifted from the bottom of the channel and flung in the air like styrofoam. The engineers were stunned and so was I. Reporters were asking questions which the engineers could not immediately answer. Everyone wondered if the dedication would have to be delayed, or worse yet, cancelled.

The engineers conducted various tests, looked at old and partial pictures of the long-gone factories for clues to the problem, and surmised that water channels created to power these factories could be the culprit. They identified the location of a water flume used to turn water wheels along the channel and filled it with concrete. They hypothesized that water pressure in that flume had caused hydrostatic pressure to push up the concrete slabs.

The engineers and construction company did another test, filled the kayak course to full capacity and crossed their fingers. Maybe they even prayed to the water gods. Then they emptied the course to see if the quick release of the water weight on the channel would hold. They left it that way for a few days and nothing happened.

We were ready for the grand opening and dedication.

A Triumph of
Imagination and Engineering

Creating a white water kayak course in downtown South Bend out of an old raceway that provided power to long gone factories was a triumph of imagination. It was also a product of ingenuity and hard work. Nonetheless, before something can happen one must imagine it.

I've known people who cannot visualize from a plan for a remodeled kitchen, a built house, or a community project. These people are sometimes said to be "mind blind" and the psychological term for this is "congenital aphantasia." I don't doubt this is true for a small percentage of the population.

Be that as it may, I believe many people who opposed the white water kayak course were more afflicted by not wanting to pay taxes for a project they thought they'd never use, or by partisan political reasons, or by a defeatist attitude toward their community.

Thankfully, the South Bend community included many citizens and leaders with vision who supported the project. The kayak course had been imagined and pushed by a group of citizens, in contrast to the ethanol plant (mentioned later in the book) suggested by two Washington lawyers. Nothing wrong with that. A community thrives when it seeks and accepts ideas from all over.

On June 29, 1983, four years from the idea being presented to me, it was time to celebrate turning a decrepit part of downtown into a beautiful reality.

Attractive bridges crossed the course where citizens could stop to view the kayakers and canoers, there were pedestrian pathways, ivy growing on the walls along the course, and movable obstructions in the water to create turbulence. People immediately marveled at the transformed area and loved it. Many who had opposed the kayak course came for the dedication and seemed to approve. Thousands attended.

It was a lot of fun. I said at the time, "We paid for this with our property and federal taxes, let's enjoy it." A gun salute touched off the activities. Three Air Force jets zoomed out of the sky in formation as I headed downstream in the whitewater course to cut the ceremonial ribbon – with two experts guiding the raft. Thank God. A few days later the Tribune called it a "charming new addition to South Bend's downtown waterfront."

All this was most gratifying. But what came immediately after was even more satisfying for me and the community. The kayak course, now called the East Race, was selected for the Mid-America Slalom series and a local competitive event was scheduled for September. In October, the U.S. Olympic Whitewater team members came from all over to practice. These events were attended by thousands lining the waterway – an audience not available at the usual water ways. The kayakers enjoyed the crowd's applause immensely.

The East Race was featured in the St. Louis Post Dispatch, the Indianapolis Star, the Fort Wayne Gazette and many national publications. The Indiana Concrete Council named the 2,000 foot waterway the Outstanding Recreation Project of the year. From a monetary investment point of view, it was highly successful almost immediately. A national company (AM General) decided to build its office along the waterway. A large apartment project later located there. An old shirt factory next to the raceway was converted into apartments. Condominiums and luxury apartments have been built. The kayak course has become a symbol of a community on the move and willing to invest in itself.

Today, many hundred million dollar projects have been built along the race, with more being developed. The Seitz Park, named in honor of James R. Seitz, Park Superintendent, who oversaw the building of the kayak whitewater course, is being transformed by the construction of a 2.5 megawatt hydroelectric plant. Additional middle and luxury apartments are being built.

Tax revenues resulting from the investment of local taxes and state and federal grants started to come in immediately. No one today would want to take the East Race away. More importantly, employers have said that they take potential employees to the East Race to encourage them to locate here.

Some people thought the kayak course was a crazy idea. No more.

Chapter 4
Learning Along
the Way

I'm Sorry
Odd Fellows Building

How do you say I'm sorry to a beautiful historic ten-story building you ordered demolished? She was a grande dame of a building in downtown South Bend which needed a facelift and internal readjustment, but no one wanted to pay for this. She was just over 50 years old and had reached that point in her life. She had fulfilled the hopes of her builders who then left her in disrepair. Now she was looking for new suitors, but those who proposed could not afford her.

She was born during the roaring 1920s through the midwifery of South Bend's elite movers and shakers, including members of the Studebaker and Oliver families. The architects, who had designed her, Freyermuth & Maurer, were Odd Fellows, and Freyermuth had been mayor of South Bend. The Odd Fellows Building represented the business and social achievements of those financially successful people.

Lest you think weird thoughts about those Odd Fellows, time takes a toll not only on buildings but on words.

The name Odd Fellows evolved from the Order of Odd Fellows founded in England during the 1700s. It was established to give aid to those in need, "to visit the sick, relieve the distress, bury the dead and educate the orphans." These people were believed to be odd because they behaved in such a selfless and seemingly impractical fashion. Indeed, they were odd in other ways. In 1851, they admitted women in the Odd Fellows Organization – the first U.S. fraternity to do so.

In 1979 the city administration planned to acquire the vacant and blighted building to demolish her. I was city council president, running for mayor at the time, and decided to take a close look at the Odd Fellows Building. Through the dust and grime of its abandoneness, I could visualize her former beauty. It contained an extraordinary banquet room for 700 people, a complete kitchen, an assembly room on the ninth floor, and a game room on the tenth floor. Then and there I decided to try to save her from the wrecking ball.

I asked the city council members to support the city's efforts to acquire the building, and to stand firmly against demolishing her to provide more time to find a way to renovate her. The council agreed and the city acquired the building, delaying her demise.

Sadly, the delay didn't produce results. Almost three years later, and two years after being elected mayor, I had failed to find a way to renovate the building and had to accept that renovation was not going to happen. On November 3, 1981, I regretfully asked the Redevelopment Commission to demolish the building. Failing to find a viable developer for the renovation of the Odd Fellows Building was one of the few disappointments of my first years as mayor.

The end didn't come easy. Preservationists continued their efforts to stop the city from demolishing the building. Nevertheless, on Friday, January 8, 1982, at 10:00 a.m., I ordered the wrecker's ball to smash into the building at the very moment when a hearing on the building's fate was to begin in the St. Joseph County Courthouse next door. A major structure built at the height of the roaring 1920s crashed to the ground in pieces. Today, the Teacher's Credit Union – one of the largest in the United States stands in its place.

Still, I'm sorry I couldn't find a way to save a grande old dame of South Bend.

Famed Architect
Philip Johnson Designs Our
Convention Center

I wanted a beautiful convention center that citizens would love for decades and would set the standard for other major buildings in South Bend and the region. It would take a world-class architect.

South Bend's business and social leaders had wanted a convention facility for decades. At last, in 1972, then Mayor Jerry Miller and a group of citizens decided to build a grand facility near the St. Joseph River in downtown South Bend. It would house a large convention hall, the South Bend Art Center and the Studebaker car collection.

This was during my first year on the city council, and it would be my first opportunity as a public servant to push for a high quality distinctive building. I knew there would be intense public pressure to select a local architect and I was convinced we should retain a world-class architect, local or not, to join with a local engineering firm for the convention center. I wanted to be a part of the decision-making group.

Right away, I asked to be appointed to the architect

selection committee. Over the years, I had developed a strong feeling that surrounding ourselves with beauty in our homes and communities would make our lives more happy, productive, and human. I'm not quite sure where all that came from, except when looking back, I see some early influences.

During my growing-up years I had developed an appreciation of fine homes by working with my father who built such homes. As a Peace Corps Volunteer in Thailand, I had been influenced by great Buddhist architecture. While in the graduate school at the University of Notre Dame, I had spent time during class breaks in what is now the Snite Museum, sitting in front of great paintings and sculptures, just looking. Soon, I was able to differentiate between great and mediocre paintings and sculptures.

We met in the County-City Building, an ugly structure which hasn't worked well since its construction in the 1960s. To this day, the building stands as a testimony to the folly of weak spine politicians who gave in to the political pressure of short-sighted community cost cutters. The building has no freight elevators, one up escalator and none to go down, and very drafty, inefficient windows. I was determined to avoid that.

The center was to be on a triangular lot next to the St. Joseph River. Many old buildings would have to be demolished, and in a real sense, a part of the city's history would be lost. I wanted the building to honor that history by dramatizing the role of the river and west raceway which had powered the city's early factories, including the Studebaker wagon works. I imagined the building as outstanding architecture, making a bold statement about the future of South Bend.

The first architectural firms selected for interviews made grand, even extravagant, presentations, sometimes with two slide projectors (no PowerPoints then). Most of them presented a square building concept, typical then of convention facilities. They did not take advantage of the triangular

61

location on the banks of the St. Joseph River, nor of the west race and the old dam adjacent to the setting.

I was not impressed, and neither were the other committee members, until we met Philip Johnson, a New York architect famous for his glass house in Connecticut. Philip Johnson was a practicing architect and an historian of architecture. He came to us with a pad and pencil – no slide projectors. He talked about the history of our downtown buildings, the courthouse, the river and his idea for our building. Drawing on his pad, taking advantage of the river, the west race, the dam, the triangular lot, he showed us what he had in mind. I was impressed by his conception of the center and his view of our city.

As a final step in the selection, we visited Johnson's office in New York City where he hosted a lunch in the famous Four Seasons restaurant he had designed, and introduced us to choreographer, Balanchine, at the Lincoln Center. That was all icing on the cake. We had already made up our minds. Our building was going to be designed by Philip Johnson.

The rest is history. South Bend has a beautiful convention building (Century Center) of which city residents are proud and to which conventioneers come back regularly. It led to other architecturally significant buildings in our downtown.

Creating a Workforce Reflecting the Diversity of Our City

When I became Mayor of South Bend in January 1980, city employees no longer reflected the demographic reality of our city. We had moved from being a city of mainly white ethnic groups to one that included many citizens of color.

In a city with an African American population of about 18 percent, only 13 percent of the work force was African American. Even more troubling, only 8 percent of police officers and 6.5 percent of firefighters were African American. Not one city department was directed by a person of color or a woman. I was determined to quickly change that.

I wasn't sure what to do, but I was not going to conduct a months-long study to assess the situation that was staring me in the face: there was discrimination based on race in hiring and promotion of city employees.

There was a useful precedent. Accommodation of ethnic groups had historically been common for hiring and promotion in the city work force. Qualifications for entry positions and promotions had usually been considered, but it had not always been a critical factor. This kind of discrimination had long been accepted as a reasonable way for the city work force to reflect the makeup of the city.

I was sure of a few things. We were not going to hire or promote anyone who was not highly qualified. We knew that if an African American person or a woman failed at a job, their race or gender would be blamed, not other factors. And we strengthened the requirements for positions to assure their relevance to the position.

Following a two-prong approach, I appointed an African American woman to lead the new human resource department and promoted an African American fire department captain to battalion chief. Meanwhile we aggressively recruited minorities for the police and fire departments.

This approach sent two powerful statements: we were serious about assuring diversity in the city's work force, and we understood that African Americans would be reluctant to work for the city if they did not see themselves in middle level and top posts.

Then, I authorized two lists from which to choose police and fire candidates for appointment – minority and non-minority lists. Whenever possible, two or three minorities were selected for each non-minority selected. We also worked to maintain the traditional ethnic balance in those departments.

I knew this was discrimination on the basis of gender and race, but I also knew we were favoring people who had been discriminated against. I was willing to push the envelope politically and legally because I knew in my gut that a diverse community cannot be governed effectively by a non-diverse work force. I was going to do this until I was forced to stop.

Eventually, the city was sued by a white applicant, which we knew would happen. We aggressively defended the suit and as expected, we lost. By then, about four years later, we had increased the percentage of African Americans in the police and fire departments to around 14 percent, not up to 18 percent reflecting the city's African population at the time, but substantial. Nothing could change that.

Additionally, the percentage of African Americans in the city work force had grown from 13 percent to 18 percent, equivalent to their numbers in the city population. When my time as mayor ended January 1, 1988, additional progress had been made and the city work force better reflected the makeup of the city. Notably, there was an African American fire chief and an African American director of the human resource department (a woman), plus 2 other women department directors.

These actions contributed substantially to a decades-long period of very little divisiveness in South Bend. In 2019, the African American percentages in police and fire were below those of 1979 – given that the city's African American population has increased from about 18 percent to around 24 percent. Furthermore, as of 2019, there was only one African American department director who doubled as the city's only woman department director.

Appointing the First
African American Fire Chief

During my first term as mayor, I set out to create a city work force that would represent the cultural makeup of South Bend. To that end I wanted to appoint an African American fire chief or police chief (or both) but that goal initially eluded me. Major institutional challenges had to be overcome to make this goal achievable.

Historic discrimination against African Americans in hiring meant that the pools of African Americans in both departments were very small. Also, once hired, African Americans were discriminated against in the allocation of special training opportunities, thus creating an even smaller group of qualified candidates for promotions. I worked to remedy those hurdles through aggressive programs and actions.

Patience is not my strong suit, still I waited for an opportunity to appoint an African American fire chief or police chief. The candidate for chief of either department would have to be exceptionally qualified, because an African American fire chief or police chief would be a first for South Bend, maybe even for Indiana. This person would be scrutinized in every way possible by their colleagues and the public. No small mistake would be easily forgiven. And the person would have to be resilient and emotionally tough.

In 1985, during my second term, an opportunity presented itself. Management problems in the fire department forced me to demote the fire chief. At that time, there were two African American battalion chiefs who were excellent candidates to be promoted chief. The longest serving battalion chief refused the promotion, but in doing so, he said, "I have just the man for you."

He recommended that the younger battalion chief, whom I had promoted in 1980, should be appointed chief. He had mentored him during his 13 years on the department and had high confidence he would be an excellent fire chief. I took his recommendation under advisement and contacted a small group of African American citizens I often asked for advice. They were thrilled I wanted to appoint an African American fire chief and agreed that the younger battalion chief should be offered the chief's position. They emphasized the excellent leadership and management skills he had exhibited as battalion chief and in the development of the department's hazardous materials handling operation. They said, "He has no 'skeletons' in his closet, is a good family man, honest to the core, is highly respected in the community, and by all factions in the fire department."

He met all, even exceeded, my criteria for a fire chief and I offered him the position. He thanked me for the offer but refused, saying, "I don't feel ready or experienced enough to take the position." I was very disappointed and suggested to my informal advisors that they urge him to reconsider my offer. Still, he wouldn't say yes.

Finally, I invited him for pizza at Rocco's - a legendary South Bend pizza place - with six or seven members of my informal advisors. They told him, "You should accept this position. You're ready for it. This is very important to the African American community. We may not have this opportunity again for a long time." He didn't say much then, but it worked. A few days later, he accepted the position.

The rest is history. Luther T. Taylor, Sr. enjoyed the longest tenure of any fire chief in the department, serving three mayors for twenty-two years. He's acknowledged to have been one of South Bend's finest fire chiefs.

Being Tone Deaf

Today, I'm physically tone deaf. I don't hear differences in the pitch of various sounds, for which I wear hearing aids. But I've always been somewhat metaphorically tone deaf in that I often miss nuances of a given situation. Regrettably, there are no hearing aids for this type of deafness which is a serious problem, especially for a politician.

During my first term as mayor an employee told me she wanted to resign her position. I knew her well, she had worked in my campaigns and was an effective employee. She said she wanted more time to take care of her father who was seriously ill. I sympathized with her and tried to make her comfortable with her decision. I said I was very sorry her father was ill and that we would miss her effective work for the city.

I fully supported her decision to resign. When an employee wants to leave a position for some reason or other, he or she should be supported in the decision and wished the best of luck. Discouraging employees from leaving and strongly encouraging them to stay may not be in their best interest nor in the best interest of the organization. Of course, understanding that can be difficult.

Later, the rumor came to me that she was quite upset because I had failed to discourage her from resigning. She felt accepting her resignation so readily was an indication I didn't value her work. Apparently, her saying she wanted to resign was her way to have me affirm her value as an employee. That thought never entered my mind at the time, and I regret my failure to understand the feelings behind her words.

I'm very direct in communicating my position on issues and my feelings to people and I tend to take the words others speak at face value. This has been both a strength and a weakness in my political and personal relationships. Maybe I project too much my way of thinking and reacting onto others.

Rumors: Good and Bad

Today rumors move at lightning speed through the internet going from one round corner of the world to another – maybe even to other planets, except we don't know if anyone is there to receive them. I suppose if there's no one to receive a rumor there's no rumor. In my political world, rumors, good and bad, always seemed to have a receptive audience.

Even before the internet, rumors moved quickly, but not at the speed of light, which provides instant gratification. Yet, I think spreading rumors before the internet was more enjoyable. It was more personal. You spread them face-to-face, or by phone, occasionally by letter.

People seem to enjoy spreading unkind rumors more than kind ones. Perhaps spreading negative rumors makes a person feel superior, and if the person receiving the rumor agrees with them, it doubles their pleasure. In my public life I enjoyed positive rumors and tried to ignore negative ones.

I remember a husband and wife who, soon after I

started my first term as mayor, took off with negative rumors about me. They had supported another candidate for the Democratic nomination for mayor. I understood their disappointment, but was surprised at their outspoken negativity towards me. Maybe I had not hired, or maybe I had fired one of their friends, but I didn't know that. We'd been friendly during my years on the city council and we had been in general agreement on the goals for our city.

Their negative comments would always come back to me quickly, sometimes the morning after an event, not quite as fast as with the internet, but fast nonetheless. People love to tell others criticism that's said about them. It's a way to ingratiate themselves with someone or to curry favor with a person, especially a public official.

The couple's bad-mouthing didn't bother me much. By then I had developed a pretty thick skin, and didn't feel a great need to approach them about it. But I knew I would see them often at political and community events, and that it might be awkward for them and for me.

Without thinking much about this, I decided to treat them in my usual friendly way. At first, they were cool toward me and didn't seem to want to talk, but I did anyway. I pretended I didn't know they were bad-mouthing me.

Whenever I saw them on the street or at an event, I'd go up to them, shake their hands, ask how they were, and do small talk. It was not my intent to change their minds. This was my way to make social situations more tolerable for them and for me.

After a year or so, their coolness seemed to mellow, and I was no longer getting reports they were making negative comments about me. Years after I had left the political arena, they always greeted me with warmth and good words about my years as mayor.

"You Don't Have the Balls to ..."

It was late at night, the meeting had gone too long, the
comments by the crossing guards had been too harsh, and
their attorney had been too full of himself. As a city council member, I was chairing a public hearing of the council
on salaries for the all-woman corps of school crossing guards
when I got "beside myself" and lost control of my words.
That's when I heard myself say in reaction to a comment by
one of the crossing guards: "You don't have the balls to . . ."

My colleagues had never heard me use this kind of
language in public, not about a group of men, and certainly
not about a group of women. They were shocked, and the
citizens in the chambers were stunned. I was apologizing profusely when the women's lawyer quickly arrived at the podium
– he practically ran to it – and blasted the hell out of me. I
deserved it.

I knew as the words were coming out of my mouth
that I shouldn't let them out, but somehow my nasty side
had taken control and gone public. While this scenario was

playing out, I felt like two persons, one nice and one nasty. The nice person in me was asking the nasty one "Why did you say that?" I had learned again, the hard way, that I will always make mistakes.

I made many small and some large mistakes during my 21 years as city councilman, mayor and school board member. When I recognized them, or as often happened, when they were pointed out to me, I apologized and tried to make up to them.

Eventually, I became more guarded and self-aware during my public discourse, and made fewer verbal blunders. Still, I knew I would always make mistakes and tried to follow the guidelines below for my apology:

1. It should be made immediately after the mistake.
2. It should be in the same context of the mistake. If the "insult" happened on television, or today on social media, the apology should be made in that medium.
3. It should be simple and direct. No excuses should be given.
4. It should include a commitment to not repeat the same mistake.

I tried to follow these guidelines, but sometimes I forgot.

Chapter 5
Building a Baseball Stadium
Downtown

What? Me Build
a Baseball Stadium?

My administrative assistant knew better than to interrupt me when I was preparing for a news conference, but that morning she did so anyway. I was a little annoyed.

Actually, I was a little bit more than annoyed because I was trying to eat my favorite honey wheat donut and drink my coffee while typing on my IBM Selectric typewriter the key points I wanted to make in a morning news conference. Typing, or keyboarding as it's called today, may well be the most important skill I learned in high school.

I would write my comments, speak them out, and time myself to make sure I got my points down to about 20 seconds. That was important for television, then the only electronic medium. Otherwise, television reporters would pick and choose from longer comments for their "show," sometimes missing key elements I wanted to communicate. Shorter comments, they tended to use whole.

My assistant said that Charlie Minkler, director of

the Michiana Area Planning Commission, wanted to talk about a baseball stadium. I had no plans to build a baseball stadium and thought the call could wait, but she said he insisted on talking with me right away. She knew politics and government from every angle and was brilliant in handling all the business of my office. I knew better than to ignore her judgment. I took the call.

Charlie told me he headed a group of baseball fans who were seeking professional baseball for South Bend. He had talked with the owners of a new Class A franchise, Robert and Debby Staley, of A. E. Staley Company fame, and John Wendel, a Florida attorney. They wanted to talk with me about locating their franchise in South Bend. The hook? South Bend would have to build a stadium. Charlie wanted me to meet with them within the next few days for they were seeing other mayors, and he was afraid they would select another city.

This was February, 1985, and building a baseball stadium was far from my mind. Actually, baseball was rarely on my mind. But Charlie was a colleague and friend, so when he urged me to meet with the franchise owners, I agreed. I saw no harm in a meeting.

No Harm in a Meeting

Even though I had never thought of building a baseball stadium in South Bend, or anywhere else, I decided to approach the meeting with an open mind. You never know what will come up, good or bad. That makes life interesting.

In the early 1980s during my first term as mayor, a group called Michiana Watershed, had proposed building a whitewater rapid kayak course in downtown South Bend, something that had not crossed my mind and seemed outlandish at the time. But I had listened to them, accepted their idea, and built a kayak course. It fast became a national and international attraction. So I listened to Charlie and the franchise owners.

I was not much of a baseball fan. As a teenager, I had listened to the World Series and attended four or five "professional" baseball games in Edmundston, New Brunswick, Canada, across the St. John River from my home in Maine. I'd even learned a few French baseball terms such as, *il mort la Poussière* – he bites the dust; *un cours circuit* – a home run.

Later, my not knowing much about baseball turned out to be useful in my quest to build the stadium. People said, "Well, at least, he's not doing this because he wants to hang out with baseball franchise owners, or with baseball players." More was made of this than was warranted. I did know the basics. But I let people have that impression, even encouraged it, because it turned out to be helpful.

During several meetings in February and March, 1985, Charlie and the franchise owners told me of the economic potential of a Class A team, about the 70 home games each season, and other events which would bring many people into downtown South Bend. They emphasized the jobs to be created, the hotel rooms to be filled, the restaurant meals to be served, and how South Bend's quality of life would be enhanced by the recreational opportunities created by a baseball stadium.

South Bend is a good sports town, not just because of Notre Dame's football, hockey, basketball, and other sports events for the community. Way back in 1860, baseball was introduced to South Bend by Henry Benjamin, known as the "Father of Baseball in South Bend." The game became popular so quickly that a 1,500 capacity stadium was built, followed by a 2,500 seat stadium in 1885. During the Second World War, the South Bend Blue Sox women's team was popular and helped take people's minds off the war. Charlie stressed, "Fans in the South Bend region will attend the games."

During these conversations, I came to appreciate the potential benefits of professional baseball for South Bend and the region, but I was not convinced those benefits would be enough to convince taxpayers to pay for a stadium. I wasn't too concerned about the possible political fallout of spending taxpayer money for a baseball stadium, however it had to stimulate economic development downtown, increase property tax revenues, and enhance the quality of life for our citizens.

The franchise owners wanted an immediate decision. They wanted to start playing in 1986, barely a year away and I was pressured to give them an answer. It had to be yes or no and it had to be very soon.

Regrettably, there was no time to fully assess and predict the economic and other benefits the owners said would accrue to the community. Nor was there time to explore the stadium as a downtown revitalization project.

People think government officials have a lot of time to make important decisions and are often criticized for making them without full knowledge. Yet, taking advantage of unexpected opportunities often requires quick decisions with little time for in-depth study. Sometimes you have to go on gut feeling and hunches honed by experience.

Another meeting was scheduled and the time had come for me to decide. I hadn't mentioned this to anyone, but lurking in the back of my mind was the idea that building a stadium as a downtown revitalization project might be worth the millions of dollars required to build a top quality stadium.

On impulse, I walked Charlie and the owners from my office to the southwest corner of the 14th floor. Looking down, I said, "If you can fit a baseball stadium between the Union Railroad Station, public housing, and a few major streets, I'll be for the project."

The group was surprised. Maybe I surprised myself too. Somehow, I had concluded in my guts, maybe in my subconscious, that building a stadium as a downtown revitalization project would be worth the money and the work required. I understood the risk for the community. It could fail. But I knew that not deciding was also risky.

On that very same day, Charlie and the director of parks measured the area, and came back excited. A baseball stadium would fit in the area I had depicted. The City Attorney said, "I guess we're building a baseball stadium."

On March 6, 1985, with no time for prior public discussion, I announced my decision to build a stadium in downtown South Bend.

The Fun Had Just Begun

I t was one thing to say that South Bend was going to build
a stadium. It was quite another to find the money to do
so. I did not fully realize the funding, legal, and political
challenges ahead even though I had faced many in building
a kayak course downtown and in attracting a $400 million
ethanol plant to the city during my first term as mayor.

The initial public reaction to my announcement that
the city was going to build a baseball stadium was favorable.
Baseball fans were enthusiastic. Ten billboards paid for by
friends of the stadium were prominent throughout South
Bend, and others made unsolicited small contributions to
help with construction costs. Baseball fans wrote letters of
support to the South Bend Tribune, and the Chamber of
Commerce endorsed the stadium. Only one council member
refused to support it.

Soon though, opposition developed, something I had
expected, but not to the extent it did. Going from the idea of
a stadium to an immediate public announcement had given
no time for even the most rudimentary planning. Cost estimates for the stadium kept going up due to delays in securing

funding, lawsuits, and my insistence on a first-class facility. During early planning, I authorized a stadium foundation of sufficient strength to support additional seating in the future, skyboxes, and a stadium club - firsts for a minor league stadium. Some who opposed the stadium said they would be for it if it cost less, which would have required cutting corners. I opposed that. A beautiful and practical stadium built for present and future use would attract fans and become a great asset to the city. If I was going to build a baseball stadium, it would be the best in the United States.

Construction cost estimates periodically going up presented a serious political challenge. Some citizens claimed I was misleading them on purpose. That was not true, but there was little I could do to change their perception. I was not happy about the increase, but making a necessary quick decision led to this difficult hand I was dealt, or had dealt to myself.

The local Republican leadership saw a political opening and got involved, mainly through a group called Fair Tax, Inc. Many of their members had actively campaigned against me in my city council and mayoral elections. They collected funds to support their crusade against the stadium, and sued the city. When I challenged them to make their membership public, they refused. They had no legal obligation to do so, but WSBT television said they were not living up to the "fair" in their name.

It got to be very nasty. Fair Tax spread rumors about my family owning land where the stadium was going to be located, all untrue. Still, all I could do was tell the truth, and seek funds for the stadium.

In spite of the nastiness and political cost, I persisted. I had promised the franchise owners we would build a stadium, and to me a promise is one you fulfill no matter how difficult it might be. Furthermore, I had become convinced that professional baseball in downtown South Bend would more than justify putting up with the nastiness.

Bar Tax? Sell a Bond?
Sign a Lease?

Finding money for a baseball stadium was an almost insurmountable challenge. City government was in a strait jacket financially, not due to wasteful spending, but dictated by statute and other state government controls.

At first I thought private donors would help, but I learned early that potential major donors were not interested in giving to build a baseball stadium. My next idea was to build the stadium with revenues from a food and beverage tax.

So on March 6, 1985, when I announced the city would build a baseball stadium, I proposed a one percent county-wide tax on food and beverage sold in restaurants and similar facilities. The challenge: this tax would have to be approved by the state legislature and the governor.

My one percent tax met stiffer opposition than I had expected. Even my county's state legislators were against it. A powerful Democratic state legislator representing South Bend opposed my proposal. I'm not sure but I believe his opposition to the one percent tax stemmed from my support of a candidate who had defeated his father for the State Senate years earlier. The prognosis for what became known as the "Parent bar tax" was bleak. I had to come up with another way for the money.

Borrow Money for a Stadium?

Knowing the food and beverage tax was dying a slow death, we had begun preparing to borrow money by selling a park bond for the stadium. On May 15, 1985, I announced we would rely on a $3.7 million bond, plus stadium revenues and other funds to build the stadium, now estimated at $4.9 to $5.65 million.

Securing local approval for the bond was not a sure thing, given that the legal process for a bond was stacked against city government. As mentioned earlier, to issue a bond in Indiana, city governments had to garner more signatures on a petition than the opposition. This made it easy to defeat a bond.

Immediately after the announcement, Mrs. Stanley Coveleski, spouse of the late Stanley Coveleski – a Baseball Hall of Famer who had lived in South Bend – launched the petition drive from her home on the near west side of South Bend. I had earlier secured her permission to name the stadium in honor of Stanley Coveleski.

Meanwhile we were moving forward with construction plans for the stadium. Funds were approved for the land survey and appraisal of properties where the stadium was to be located. The architectural firm, Hellmuth, Obata & Kassabaum of Kansas City, and the engineering firm of Cole Associates had been retained, and preliminary designs for the stadium had been prepared.

I knew it was risky to spend money for a stadium

which might never be built – money earmarked for other city needs. We could be left with a deep hole in the ground. Many of my friends and supporters thought I was committing political suicide.

I wasn't too worried, however my staff was acutely concerned that no matter how many signatures we got, the opposition could get more after we filed the petitions. Then I too became concerned, and feared we might not prevail.

By late August, 1985, I knew our bond was in trouble. It would be a huge gamble to file the petition, lose and have to deal with the resulting negative publicity. Yet, it would be equally negative to not file the petitions, and look for an as-yet-unknown way to fund the stadium.

What to do? I felt we were coming to the end of our funding rope. I had to make a decision. It came down to my not wanting a second defeat. I had lost my "bar tax" due to negative legislators, and I didn't want to lose the bond due to local naysayers. I decided to not file our petitions.

I had rolled the dice with no clue of the next step. Still, I was confident there was a way to find money for the stadium. The challenge was to find it. That's what I told the City Attorney and the director of economic development.

Bypass the Public – Lease Purchase Agreement

"Strike two on Parent" was the word around town. The opposition was emboldened and we were disheartened. Still we were determined to find a way.

My staff came to me with only one possibility – one they were not satisfied with. They said we should try to secure funds through a lease purchase arrangement with a financial institution.

Family Victory: Left to right, Mayor Roger Parent, Michelle Parent, Rolande Parent, Denise Parent. Front, Melissa Parent, Noel Parent, 1980.

Campaigning.
From left to right: Rolande Parent,
Roger Parent, 1983

Rolande Parent, woman behind the scenes. To her right, Mayor Roger Parent, circa 1986

From left to right: Debbie Urbanski, Roger Parent, Bob Urbanski, Rolande Parent, Michelle ParentThesing, Bill Murphy, Senator Donnelly, Mayor Pete Buttigieg, Andrew Berlin, South Bend Cubs Owner, and his children.
Courtesy South Bend Cubs

Four Winds Field at Coveleski Stadium.
Courtesy, South Bend Cubs 2021

Richard Hill was South Bend's first full time City Attorney (Corporation Counsel) 1980 – 1986. He pioneered changes in the police department, had a major role in the ethanol plant, the East Race kayak course, the Coveleski Stadium, and more. He drafted legislation that became major tools for the redevelopment of Indiana communities

From Left to Right: Andrew Berlin, South Bend Cubs owner, honoring former Mayor Roger Parent, builder of the Coveleski Stadium now Four Winds Field, at its 30th anniversary.
Courtesy South Bend Cubs

Stanley Coveleski, Baseball Hall of Famer. South Bend's minor league stadium named in his honor.

Bob Hope joking with Mayor Roger Parent: "You want to build a minor league stadium in downtown South Bend?" circa 1985 at Pat's Colonial Pub in Mishawaka.

Mayor Parent at bat. Ground Breaking of the Coveleski Stadium (Now Four Winds Field) 1986

Luther Taylor, Sr., South Bend's first African American Fire Chief, 1985

Charles T. Hurley, Police Chief circa 1986.

Cathy (Hubbard) Grundy-Davis, first woman director of newly established Human Resource Department, circa 1983

Eugenia Schwartz, first woman City Attorney of South Bend. 1986-87

Kathy Barnard, first Woman Director of Code Enforcement Department 1985-86

Patricia DeClercq, Director, Code Enforcement Department 1986-87

International Special Olympics, University of Notre Dame Stadium and South Bend, Mayor Roger Parent and Rolande Parent with world participants. 1987.

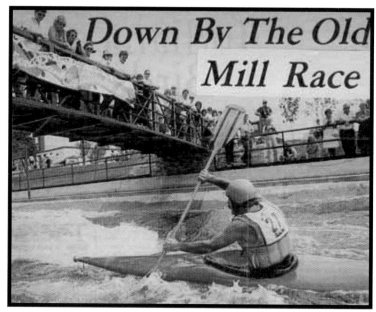

Enjoying the new downtown South Bend white water course. 1984

James (Jim) Seitz, Superintendent, South Bend Parks.
Seitz Park at the East Race, dedicated in his honor, 1984.

Dancing the polka
while campaigning
on South Bend's
west side, circa, 1983

*Peace Corps Volunteer Roger Parent (second from right)
fishing with Thai teachers, circa 1962*

*India World Dignity
program kids with Roger
Parent, circa 2018*

Roger Parent,
circa 2018

Mayor Parent answering questions
asked by fifth graders, circa 1984

Building home with tsunami victims in Thailand, 2005

Sargent Shriver,
Peace Corps Direc-
tor, American
Ambassador to
Thailand with
students at the
Technical School in
Thailand where
I taught as a
Volunteer. 1962.

The lease purchase approach had the attractive virtue of avoiding a local remonstrance by citizens - it could not be defeated with signatures. But citizens could and would lobby the members of the Indiana Local Property Tax Control Board and the Board of Tax Commissioners who had to approve the lease. These two groups, appointed by a Republican governor, would be under tremendous pressure to vote against the lease.

I was willing to take that on and authorized this plan immediately. We had no other plan. I had no choice.

In late September 1985, I announced that a lease purchase arrangement was being developed with Security Pacific of San Francisco. The city would pay the lease through a combination of cable fees, stadium revenues, and property taxes. Security Pacific would own the stadium for 10 years after which it would be deeded to the city.

Needless to say, this tactic further enraged and energized opposition to the stadium. They called it undemocratic and felt I was not listening to them, which was true. I knew this was right for South Bend and I was not going to give in to the short-term views of what had become a large number of citizens - maybe even a majority.

State Republican Support
for the Lease? Secret Meeting?

Would the Republican dominated Local Property Tax Control Board and Tax Commission approve the lease? That was the big question. Without their approval, the stadium was dead.

I was not sure how to get this crucial Republican support and neither was my staff. We knew opponents of the stadium would contact members of those boards, and that the members were well aware of the stadium controversy in South Bend. Equally important, the stadium issue had become entangled with the leadership of the local Republican Party.

On a Friday after work, we went to Rocco's, our favorite pizza place, for a beer or two. Too much beer can dull the senses, but sometimes it can heighten the imagination. The City Attorney came up with the idea we should approach Governor Robert Orr directly and ask for his support. He felt that if Governor Orr was supportive, he might be willing to influence board members to approve the stadium. This approach could be risky. Losing the governor's support up front could doom the lease even before the board hearings.

Still, I liked the idea. I was reminded of my Peace Corps Volunteer work in rural Thailand decades earlier. Before visiting villagers to discuss a project, I would first meet with the village chief (Phujai Ban) and the senior Buddhist monk. This was the best way to get the cooperation of the villagers. If the governor was even mildly supportive, this might favorably dispose his appointees toward our lease proposal. "Let's do it," I said.

We hired an Indianapolis law firm politically close to the governor to set up the meeting, which they promptly did. There was to be no publicity about this meeting, something we readily agreed to. Any publicity would have been counterproductive.

Secret Meeting with the Governor

Around January 1986 - I don't remember the exact date -we had our secret meeting with Governor Orr. By that time, the lease agreement had been fully negotiated, and the franchise owners had announced that the White Sox were interested in being the parent club of the South Bend franchise, good news we could bring to our meeting.

The president of the Redevelopment Commission (an influential former Republican congressman) the local Chamber of Commerce, the Park Board and a few other supporters of the stadium joined me in the meeting.

Governor Orr, a down-to-earth informal person, made us feel very welcomed. I was surprised to see the three tax commissioners present, indeed a good omen. We outlined the potential benefits of the stadium for our downtown, the business community, and the quality of life. The governor and his staff asked a few questions. So did the tax commissioners. At the end of our short meeting, the governor said, "this appears to be a good project." That's all.

I had not expected him to say the project should be approved, but for him to say it was a good project was encouraging. We had accomplished what we'd set out to do. The project was now in the hands of the Local Property Tax Control Board which would recommend yes or no to the Tax Commission which was not required to accept their recommendation.

As we left, our Indianapolis attorney said, "this meeting never happened."

Will the Lease be Approved by the Tax Commissioners?

We had done all we could with Governor Orr. Now we had to continue countering the negative and false publicity being spread by Fair Tax, Inc. and other naysayers.

On January 13, 1986, the Local Property Tax Control Board recommended that the tax commissioners deny the lease. I was disappointed with the negative recommendation, still I knew that the tax commissioners did not have to follow their recommendation.

A few weeks later, the three-member tax commission approved the lease by a two to one vote, to the great consternation of Fair Tax. We were ecstatic, but that was short-lived. Additional hearings were scheduled in South Bend which gave the impression that their decision could be reversed with additional information. I think this was a sop given to the opposition.

Finally, on May 1, the tax commissioners affirmed their positive decision on the lease and we thought we could get the funds. But this was not to be. Fair Tax, Inc. filed a number of lawsuits, one in the Circuit Court which was followed, finally, by the State Supreme Court dismissing the matter on September 4.

Funds were released on September 1986, and on that day we held the official ground breaking ceremony between pylons in the hole dug for the stadium. The celebration was small – much work remained.

Staleys Sell the Franchise: "Crazy" Mayor Won't Talk

I was enjoying my 25th class reunion banquet at St. Francis Xavier University in Nova Scotia, when I was handed a note to call the City Attorney. There were no cell phones then and so I looked for a pay phone. I wondered what was so urgent that he would interrupt me during one of my infrequent absences from the city. It had to be important.

"What's up?"

"They sold the franchise." I could tell he was upset.

"The Staleys and Wendel sold the franchise to Jay Acton and Eric Margenau of New York City. I've talked with them but they insist on talking with you without delay. That's why I called you." I was stunned.

This was early Fall 1986. Stadium funding had been secured and construction on the Coveleski Stadium was going full blast, even under night lights. Due to many delays, the stadium would not be completed until summer 1987, but this was something the franchise owners had accepted. In 1987 they were going to play in Daytona Beach.

We'd have to begin negotiating an operating agreement with the new owners from scratch. An existing agreement could have made it more difficult for the New York owners to move the franchise to another city. However that was not likely since the new owners would need a place for their team and we were building the finest Class A baseball stadium in the USA – downtown, with sky boxes, a grand club, and many other amenities.

The City Attorney's call was urgent for several reasons. There would be serious political fallout to handle, and the New York owners had demanded to talk with me immediately.

To say I was upset would be a large understatement. I was in no mood to talk with them or anyone else about the situation. "Tell the new owners I don't want to talk with them."

I'm not sure why the Staleys and Wendel decided to sell the franchise. Probably, they had not understood the public process of getting funding, and got tired of the nastiness, or they wanted an immediate profit. They had paid $20,000 for the franchise and had sold it for $455,000 without having played one season.

By the time I had returned home, Fair Tax and other naysayers had intensified their criticism of my decision to build a stadium, saying it would turn out to be a very expensive white elephant which would be a burden on taxpayers. This was not an easy time.

On November 2, 1986, the sale was approved by the Midwest League and I was still refusing to take phone calls from the new owners. They kept asking the City Attorney if I was crazy.

Is the Mayor Crazy?

The new owners, Jay Acton and Eric Marganau, probably wondered if they had bought a pig-in-a-poke. Were they dealing with a certifiably crazy mayor? Was that why the Staleys and Wendel had sold the franchise?

"Why is the mayor refusing to talk with us?" they asked the City Attorney. "He's got a half-built stadium, millions of taxpayer dollars spent, and he refuses to talk. What's the matter with him?"

Actually, the City Attorney was talking with the new owners and had started the ground work for an operations agreement. It wasn't going to be easy to get the best possible deal for the city because we had lost leverage when the franchise was sold without an operating agreement.

But we were lucky. My emotional reaction of not talking with the new owners had created leverage for the city. Totally unplanned, we had stumbled upon a great negotiating strategy. I was the crazy mayor while the City Attorney was the reasonable guy working hard to negotiate a fair agreement for the city that he might be able to convince me to accept.

In his book, Green Diamonds, (p. 85) Acton expresses his view about my not talking with them:

". . .When Eric Margenau and I came in the picture after buying the team from the original owners, Parent was – and this was most puzzling to me – playing hardball. At first he just refused to talk to us. He threatened that he didn't have to talk to us, or to anyone else for that matter, and that if all they played in the new park was American Legion ball, that was okay with him. He did of course eventually start to talk to us, thanks in large part to the efforts of Rich Hill.

". . .Hill and Parent fought the good fight, and got a good deal for the city of South Bend."

The operational agreement we negotiated with the new owners became a model agreement used by many cities and franchise owners as a basis for their operation.

Play Ball! Reaching the Vision for the Stadium and Downtown Development

E arly in 1987, as the final touches were being put on the Stanley Coveleski Regional Stadium, the criticism melted away. The stadium stood in all its beauty, a new vision for downtown South Bend. It had acquired a nickname: the Cove.

It was time to play ball.

- "Parent Didn't Strike Out," wrote the Tribune, May 14, 1987.
- "I will attend games," said Janet Allen, first woman to run for mayor, a Republican icon, who had opposed the stadium. "It's beautiful."
- "The Cove put the City on the map," wrote Bill Moor, South Bend Tribune Columnist, July 10, 1987.
- "We're proud of the stadium," said the South Bend Tribune, August 3, 1987.

The Stanley Coveleski Stadium was dedicated August 25, 1987. Mrs. Stanley Coveleski, now in her 90s attended. So did Charlie Minkler who had planted the seed for the stadium.

Meanwhile, pending the White Sox farm club playing in 1988, the stadium was being fully used. People, young and old enjoyed the games and activities. The Cove hosted:

- The NCCAA baseball tourney with Bethel college.
- Some Pan Am exhibition games.
- Soccer games during the 1987 International Special Olympics.
- The Legion Post 50's Marauder Mixer Tourney.

On April 10, 1988, my wife, Rolande, threw the ceremonial first pitch at the first South Bend White Sox game. By then I was Peace Corps Director in Haiti and Joe Kernan was mayor.

The franchise made money for the owners and the city. In its very first year, they made a profit of $50,000 and in 1989 they realized $400,000. Each year saw record attendance and the stadium lease was fully paid in 10 years.

Some South Bend citizens had thought I was crazy for building a baseball stadium. Maybe what's seen as crazy by some people is not so crazy after all. Just something they couldn't imagine.

A New Era:
Andrew T. Berlin Rejuvenates
the Team and the Area

In 2011, Andrew Berlin, CEO of Berlin Packaging, acquired the team and brought his large vision for the stadium and the team to South Bend. He knew the Cove and the baseball team could do much more for our community and he immediately set to work.

Over the years, the franchise had lost some of its pizzaz. The city had invested in the stadium to keep it in good shape, but it needed certain amenities to keep up with the changing expectations of the fans.

Berlin set out immediately to create excellence in his team. In January 2012, he introduced Joe Hart as the team's new president of the Silver Hawks. Hart had just been named Florida State League Executive of the Year.

Working hand-in-hand with city officials, a new phase of improvements and additions was initiated. Berlin committed $8.0 million of his money and the city added $1.75 million for other amenities.

The 2012 season marked 25 years of professional

baseball in South Bend and the start of a new era. Under Berlin's ownership, the franchise increased its attendance by 68 percent over the previous year. The next season saw a record attendance and the stadium's five millionth fan passed through its gates.

In 2014, Andrew announced that the team had changed its name to South Bend Cubs. The team had become an affiliate of the Chicago Cubs to the delight of all South Bend. Andrew Berlin did not rest on these laurels. He had many more ideas and plans.

• 2015 – Grand opening of the South Bend Cubs Performance Center.
• 2015 – Baseball Digest named the South Bend Cubs their Team of the Year.
• 2016 – Extension of the relationship with the Chicago Cubs through 2030 season.
• 2016 – Won the John H. Johnson Award as America's premier minor-league team.
• 2017 – Broke ground for a $23 million mixed use residential housing. Four Winds Field named Ballpark Digest's best single-A ballpark.
• 2021 – Announced a major expansion and upgrade to the stadium. Will add an upper deck, new scoreboard, and improved lighting. South Bend elevated to High-A affiliate with Chicago Cubs – partners to 2030.

The excitement generated by Andrew Berlin and his South Bend Cubs has been a large influence in redeveloping the Southwest side of downtown South Bend and has enhanced the entire community.

What I imagined in 1985, Andrew Berlin is making real today.

Role of the Media
and the Stadium

My proposal for a baseball stadium in South Bend
had top billing in the news for the two years of
planning and construction. At one point, the South
Bend Tribune said the stadium had been the most controversial and divisive issue in the community since the 1950s water
fluoridation issue. Bill Moor, a sports columnist for the South
Bend Tribune, wrote, "This baseball story is really 'off the
wall,'" arguing it should be made into a movie with Dustin
Hoffman portraying me. Looking back on it, I barely know
how my mild-mannered, low-key self became so controversial.

In the 1980s, the media in South Bend included
television, radio, and the Tribune. Together, they had a large
influence on the public life of the community, especially the
Tribune which had a large circulation and took editorial positions on major issues, and some not so major.

I met often with the Tribune editorial board throughout the two-year-long stadium project to inform them and to
gain their support. In spite of that, the Tribune's editorial

support wavered from strong to weak to strong. On May 5, 1985, just a few months after the decision to build the stadium, the Tribune had a positive editorial titled "Play Ball." Six months later, they editorialized that the city "should ask itself if a baseball stadium is the best investment among many other needs." A year later after stadium funding had been secured, they wrote "Go Ahead and Build."

Rumors had it that the Tribune's retired publisher had a driver who had been a popular softball pitcher for a national champion South Bend team and that he opposed the stadium. Apparently, he had convinced the publisher that the stadium was not a good idea. So whenever the publisher went to his part time office, his opposition was reflected in an editorial. When he stayed away, the editorial board took a more positive stance toward the stadium.

Although the editorial board wavered on the stadium, it was clear to me that many Tribune reporters and columnists were very positive about it. This was reflected in their news and columnist articles. Sports reporters were supportive and Jack Colwell, a well-known reporter and respected columnist, told me years later that he had been authorized to assess the impact of Class A baseball in a variety of communities. His extensive articles on the positive economic and quality of life impact of Class A baseball had a large influence on the readership and the Tribune editorial board. I believe his articles were decisive in changing the opinions of many citizens and members of the editorial board, for which I am very thankful.

Chapter 6
Threatening to Kill
the Mayor

"I'm Going to Kill the Mayor"

"I'm going to kill the mayor," the phone caller said. During my first year as mayor in 1980, the former Evansville, Indiana, mayor, had been shot to death by a mentally ill woman upset over having her home inspected by city workers. And in January, 1982, Laporte, Indiana, Mayor A. J. Rumely, Jr. and his wife were killed in their LaPorte home by a disgruntled former city employee who had been fired days earlier.

This latest incidence of violence against a mayor, just a half hour from South Bend, had prompted the police department to establish a procedure to keep someone who threatened to harm me on the phone long enough to trace the call. They also gave me a police radio and installed a security system in my home. Although I was concerned about my safety and that of my family, it never was at the forefront of my mind. Like most mayors, I relished being accessible to citizens.

One place where I asked for police protection was in parades. Parades in South Bend are often on narrow streets where you can almost touch the viewers. Sometimes they ran up to shake my hand. Once, a viewer close to me, about 15 feet away, stared long and hard at me with such deep hatred in his eyes that it bothered me. Just writing about it today makes me shiver.

There was real cause for concern. Once, a person tried to get into my home in the middle of the night. Even after I turned on the lights, he broke through the storm door and tried to break down the main door. He seemed determined to enter and cause us harm. It was very scary for our four children, my wife and me. Fortunately, the police arrived just in time to catch him in the act. Turned out he was intoxicated and thought he was at his girlfriend's house. He had a job he would have lost had I pressed charges, which I didn't have the heart to do.

Back to the man on the phone. My secretary kept him talking long enough to trace the call to a phone booth on the southwest side of the city, and the police were able to apprehend him. His story was that the water to his basement apartment had been cut off, he had lost his job, his wife was ill, he had five children, and there was no food left in the apartment. He was a desperate father and husband trying to get help for his family. The police called my office to find out what to do with him. All they could legally do was admonish him and keep him on their "radar."

When I learned of this man's situation, I wondered what I would have done had I been in his shoes. I too would have been very desperate and might even have done what he did. Who knows? We decided to help him. I asked the police to hold him at the station while I and my staff figured out how we could help. We got him a temporary job with the park department, restored the water to his apartment, and got my church food pantry to bring food and a little cash to tide the family over until he got his first pay check. And we went after the landlord whose responsibility it was to pay the water bill.

The ability to help a family in trouble gave me more satisfaction than many of my other responsibilities. I worried however about others in similar circumstances who would never threaten to commit some desperate act to get support that society should provide as a matter of course.

"No Wonder You Were Burglarized, You Live in a Bad Neighborhood"

That's what a South Bend police officer told a citizen who was reporting a burglary when I was President of the city council in 1976.

I was very upset by this comment and immediately filed a bill with the city council requiring all new employees to live in the city and forbidding those currently living in the city from moving out. The bill got spirited opposition, especially by police and fire associations, who eventually filed suit in court. Nonetheless, the city council supported the bill and it became law.

I admit, it sounds somewhat un-American to force city employees to live in the city they serve. Shouldn't city employees have the freedom to live where they choose? Some might think this a constitutional right. I was a little conflicted about filing the bill, but I felt that the police officer's insensitive view of my city was generated to some extent by his being out of touch with city residents.

I was determined to use every tool I had to counter that view. No one is required to work for a city, but if they do,

I feel they should live in the city they wish to serve. City residents desire to be served by employees who live among them, they don't want their laws and regulations enforced by people who don't have to live under those laws and regulations.

It's a deeply felt American principle that those who rule should live in the areas they serve. How else can they have intimate knowledge of and sensitivity to the needs of their citizens? This is why most elected officials in the United States are required to live in the jurisdictions they serve. (U.S. Representatives have to live in the state, but not in their district.) South Bend police and firefighters eventually won their court suit because the Indiana legislature had given them special dispensation from local residency laws, allowing them to live up to 15 miles outside the city limits. Interestingly, they did not give that right to other city employees, thus creating two different classes of city employees, something which may be unconstitutional.

That some people want a city job but don't want to live in the city tells me they lack an essential element required of a city worker – the willingness to support the city financially and personally, and to know the pleasures and challenges of living in that city. Employees living in the city strengthen neighborhoods, contribute to the tax base from which they benefit, and have a greater personal stake in their community. Why wouldn't they want to live in the city they serve?

Maybe it's more un-American for city employees to come from outside to rule over city residents than to require them to live in the city.

City Worker Pees on the Street and Police Officer Farts in his Radio

Bizarre stuff happens.

A street department worker peed on the street behind his department truck where he was filling potholes, and a mother of many kids saw him through her picture window. She called the police who cited him for indecent exposure. His excuse: "I had to pee and had no place to go." Turns out he had a kidney problem and really had to go right away.

There was no "Joy John" nearby and it was pee on the street or pee in his pants – a real dilemma. I'm not sure what I would have done in his situation. Maybe just as he did. Anyway, the city's compassionate legal department got involved, and the woman, after a full explanation of the situation, dropped her complaint. His foreman gave him an assignment closer to restroom facilities.

****

The fart incident is comical but even more bizarre. An unknown police officer had farted in his radio and disrupted police radio traffic. I couldn't help myself and laughed when

I found out about it. If the officer had only farted once in his radio, the chief might have laughed it off too. But the officer had farted in his radio on many occasions during a two-month period and the chief had to do something about it.

This was no laughing matter even though the whole department was laughing. Still, rules have to be followed, particularly when police radio communications are being disrupted, even by a police officer's farts. It had become a public safety issue and could easily have become widely known, which the police chief wanted to avoid.

The first challenge was to find the culprit. Through a fine piece of detective work using modern police techniques (that's what the detectives said), he was found. Actually, once the police administration decided to do something about this, it didn't take long to figure out which officer on the evening shift would be most likely to engage in this kind of childish behavior. They quickly found their man.

The chief wanted the punishment to be one administered privately to avoid embarrassment for the officer and the department, so he suspended him with pay for a few days. But as hard as it is to believe this – although it shouldn't be, given the culprit's stupid behavior – the officer refused this very light punishment, and contested it in the public forum of the Public Safety Board. It made him and the city a public joke on local and Chicago talk radio for days.

A Python is Loose in the City

A huge pet python had escaped its cage on the porch of a house on the near east side of South Bend and was roaming the neighborhood. Rumors put it at 15 to 20 feet long and weighing some 50 pounds, but really it was about 10-feet long and weighed much less than 50 pounds. What's more, it was certainly not slithering throughout the 40 square miles of South Bend. A python can move only about five miles per hour at its fastest. But I didn't know that then, nor did most people.

Citizens were alarmed. Hundreds of telephone calls were jamming the police lines and keeping my staff busy. Something's got to be done. Catch it. Kill it. Do something. Now. But when police officers reached the scene of a snake sighting, the snake had disappeared. There were no cell phones in those days. What was I to do? To most people, this had become a serious public safety concern – perhaps an exaggeration, but perception is reality. After a month of snake sightings the police chief issued an order to destroy the snake on sight.

I'm not afraid of snakes, but I don't go looking

for them either. I had seen snakes up close during my Peace Corps service in Thailand and had heard the story of a missionary sister from Michigan who had killed "with her bare hands" a boa constrictor that had fallen on her desk from the school rafters. I'd even gone to see the dead snake in the school. I knew that pythons, under certain circumstance, could be dangerous to adults, let alone small children. I supported the chief's decision.

Very early one morning, around 12:30 a.m., an off-duty police officer saw the snake crossing Jefferson Boulevard and drove over it with his private vehicle. Twice he did this with no apparent effect on the snake. When the snake headed for shrubbery, he called for backup. Then he jumped out of his car, opened the trunk, grabbed his department-issued shotgun and shot the snake three times. When the snake reared up its head, he shot it a fourth time.

Backup arrived and that officer, for good measure, shot it a fifth time. By then, a South Bend Tribune photographer had arrived on the scene, taken pictures of the snake and asked the on-duty officer in his uniform to hold the snake over his head in a victory pose, promising it would not be published – he would give him the picture. But next day, this victory-posed picture of the police officer with a silly grin on his face made the front page of the South Bend Tribune.

Citizens were relieved, but the phone calls to my office and the chief's didn't end. We were getting chastised by snake and animal lovers, including the city's zoo keeper who said that the snake was not very dangerous and could have been captured. "I should have been called," he said. Where were all those people when the snake was "roaming" the city? And piling insult on injury, the grieving pet snake owner threatened to sue the city for killing his pet snake.

Later, an elementary class from a Catholic school

brought a letter to the police chief deploring the killing of the snake.

This story lasted days on talk radio here and in Chicago.

Chapter 7
Building an Ethanol Plant in the City

An Ethanol Plant Was Not a Campaign Promise

I n my campaign for mayor in 1979, I had promised good streets, quick snow removal, clean water, and effective economic development. An ethanol plant in the city hadn't even crossed my mind.

I was mayor-elect in the middle of organizing my administration and preparing to deal with city issues that would be on my plate January 1, 1980. It was a hectic time. But when U.S. Congressman John Brademas (D) Third District, now Second and U.S. Senator Birch Bayh (D) telephoned, I gladly took their calls. Their political clout and savvy were very important to South Bend. Moreover, they had supported my campaign for mayor and I had worked in their campaigns.

Congressman Brademas, the powerful Majority Whip of the House, and the influential Senator Bayh were good friends of South Bend. When they asked me to meet with two Washington, D.C. lawyers who were planning to build an ethanol plant, I immediately agreed. Senator Bayh said he wanted the plant in Indiana and Congressman

Brademas wanted it in his district. And I was interested in discussing this project for South Bend.

I was intrigued and excited by the possibility of attracting a multimillion dollar project that would create new jobs, add to South Bend's tax base, and expand the market for corn grown in the area. And given my growing-up-days in Maine farm country, I thought this would be a unique way to strengthen city – farm economic ties.

The two D.C. lawyers, Barry Direnfeld and Don Evans, called me the same day of my conversations with Brademas and Bayh. They were in a rush and eager to meet, which we did a few days later in South Bend. They said, "We can build the plant in any state that grows a lot of corn, or anywhere in Indiana, but we seek your help to build it in South Bend." I promised my full support.

They openly acknowledged their reasons for Indiana, the Third Congressional District, and South Bend. They needed congressional action to make the ethanol plant happen, something Senator Bayh and Congressman Brademas had promised. Both were running for re-election in 1980 and building the plant in predominantly Democratic South Bend would help solidify their base. Barry said they would require city, county, and state legislative action no matter where it was built, and would need a local elected official to take the lead in coordinating these efforts. That's where I came in the picture.

My decision to support the ethanol plant was a no brainer. We were in a recession, unemployment was high and I had promised a strong economic development program. Building the plant would generate an investment of nearly $600 million in 2020 dollars, create 600 construction jobs, 140 permanent jobs and hundreds more indirectly. It would use 20 percent of the corn crop in the region and add millions of dollars to the city's tax base.

I said yes, not knowing what would come next, but I would soon find out after taking office as mayor.

Slogging in the Muck

A few days after being sworn in as mayor on January 1, 1980, I was slogging in the muck of farm fields south of South Bend with my new friends, Don and Barry. It doesn't take long to become friends when big dollars are involved, for them and for the city. They had their dress shoes on, but I was wearing farmer's boots. I had worked on farms in northern Maine and knew how mucky good rich top soil is like when wet.

I was immersed in the search for a 70-acre site for the ethanol plant because the complicated process involved the city first acquiring the property and eventually transferring it to Barry and Don, or more accurately, to their New Energy Corporation. The preferred parcel was owned by an elderly widow. I was designated to meet with her, the idea being she might respond better to me than to the D.C. lawyers. It also made sense since the city was acquiring the property.

The meeting didn't go well. She was not interested in selling even though a premium price was being offered – one that would not likely be matched any time soon. I met often with her, but to no avail. She would not sell her land at any price. Her attachment to the land and all the memories it raised in her were very strong. I was disappointed, but sympathized with her. Money is far from everything and memories are part of one's life – especially when one is older.

There was no time to waste. New Energy planned to start constructing the plant in 1982. Given the lead time to design the plant and to develop funding which would involve banks, federal, state and local governments, we had to find a site immediately.

Meanwhile, Barry said they were exploring other cities in Indiana to locate their plant. I'm not sure I believed this, but I didn't blame them for covering all their bases. They were putting extra pressure on me and that was quite all right. I work well under pressure.

We kept slogging through the mucky spring farm fields seeking a suitable place for the plant. We found a 70-acre parcel owned by someone I knew well since I had opposed the purchase of his water and sewer utility company by the city when I was president of the city council. There was no love lost between us, but money spoke louder to him than for the widow who wouldn't sell her land at any price. He quickly accepted the premium price offered for his land.

After nailing down the site, the city promised Barry and Don tax abatement, construction of access roads, and submission of applications for federal and state funds. With these commitments in hand, New Energy announced on March 17, 1980, that South Bend had been selected as the site for their ethanol plant. I was pleased but not surprised at their decision. I had thought all along, given the time they'd put into South Bend and Congressman Brademas' strong support, that South Bend was their preferred place.

During all this time, we were working non-stop for the re-election of Senator Bayh and Congressman Brademas.

Their re-election was critical to the actions required by Congress and federal agencies for the ethanol plant.

Would Congressman Brademas and Senator Bayh win or lose?

Tough Re-Election Campaigns for John Brademas and Senator Birch Bayh

Nineteen-eighty was a difficult year for Democrats across the nation, especially in Indiana – a Republican state, today more so. Then unpopular President Jimmy Carter headed the Democratic ticket. Early private polls showed that John Brademas and Birch Bayh were running substantially behind their opponents, John Hiler and Dan Quayle respectively.

We pulled out all the stops and campaigned hard for both candidates. Losing Congressman Brademas and Senator Bayh would be disastrous not only for the ethanol plant, but for the well-being of South Bend. They had been directly involved in developing and enacting legislation of great significance for our country. Having an influential senator and a powerful congressman representing South Bend in Washington helped immensely to get grants and favorable treatment.

When John Hiler invited the head of the National Chamber of Commerce to South Bend for his campaign, I struck back. In a news conference, I castigated the National

Chamber leadership and John Hiler for their insensitivity to the problems facing cities and the poor, and I reiterated my strong support for John Brademas. I had made Hiler very unhappy with me.

Regardless of my efforts and that of many other people, Brademas and Bayh lost their re-elections. I had known their chances were bleak, and I was somewhat prepared for their loss. Still I was very disappointed.

In one fell swoop, those strong proponents of ethanol and the plant for South Bend were lost. Barry Direnfeld and Don Evans might even have to move their project to another more politically favorable congressional district and state. They had already committed a lot of time and substantial resources to our area, but that was not decisive relative to the total cost of the project and the required federal actions.

Don, Barry and I had a few beers over this and decided to try to convert the ethanol plant to a Republican project. Indiana's top leadership was Republican and we thought it worth the effort to ask newly elected Congressman Hiler and Senator Dan Quayle to support the ethanol plant for South Bend. Also, I had a good relationship with Senator Richard Lugar (R) who had been a very successful mayor of Indianapolis and understood the problems of cities.

We set up meetings with Congressman Hiler and Senators Lugar and Quayle.

Will the Ethanol Plant
Survive the Election Loss?

I wondered if we would ever reach ground breaking for this multi-million dollar plant. When Senator Bayh and Congressman Brademas lost their elections, most people felt this project was doomed for South Bend. I asked myself if the hundreds of hours spent by me and the staff on a project that might never happen were justified. Other people did too.

Focusing on the ethanol plant meant less time for other critical matters. I didn't want to start as mayor by losing out on a major economic development project for which I could be blamed, even if I was blameless. It might set a negative tone that could affect future and less risky business proposals by other entrepreneurs. But no matter how difficult this project seemed and how much of a long shot it appeared to be, I was not about to give up. Giving up on a tough challenge was not in my DNA.

Reaching groundbreaking would require getting Republican support and a gargantuan organizational and coordinating effort by the city staff. Plus, support and decisions by local, state, and national officials would be needed.

The U.S. Department of Energy would have to guarantee a $140 million loan and the U.S. Senate would have to extend the four cent per gallon excise tax on gasohol. A $30 million dollar limited partnership would have to be sold and the city would have to buy $5 million of those partnerships – something never done by an Indiana city. A syndicate of banks would have to arrange a large loan for New Energy, and I would have to establish a local committee for a $1 million local fund drive.

Hundreds of elected officials and business and other community leaders would have to meet all the commitments required of local governments and the community. Finally, only after these numerous complex financial and legal knots were resolved, and these requirements were met, the questions remained whether the New Energy Corporation would be ready to begin construction.

The essential step: Getting the support of Congressman Hiler and Senators Lugar and Quayle.

Hiler Plays Hard
to Get / Lugar Takes the Lead

My vigorous opposition to John Hiler's candidacy made me somewhat apprehensive about meeting with him. Still, I needed to begin establishing a working relationship with him. There was much at stake for South Bend, not only the ethanol plant, but a wide array of activities ranging from pending federal grants, public housing funding, and federal regulations affecting our community.

Campaigning against Hiler for Brademas was a political defeat for me, but not one I regretted. No matter our different politics and how upset he may have been about my role in the campaign, we were elected to serve many of the same people, South Bend being the largest city in his district.

Initially, Congressman Hiler appeared disinterested in meeting with me. My staff's attempts to set a meeting kept getting ignored and delayed. Maybe it was his way of showing he was in control and had power. Or maybe I was too anxious. Who knows? I'd already sent him a letter of congratulations, and I was very willing to eat humble pie. Finally, I called and persuaded his staff to schedule a meeting. I offered to meet in his office in Laporte, Indiana, where he lived, but they said he would be in South Bend and meet in my office. I thought it was a good sign that he would meet me on my turf.

There were almost no introductory pleasantries. I congratulated him again on his victory which he barely acknowledged. Instead, he emphasized his strong victory over Brademas and me, more than hinting that if I opposed him again, he would take action. I didn't know what he meant by that and didn't ask. I had been elected mayor by a big margin in a largely Democratic city. He couldn't be much of a political threat to me. Maybe he was alluding to the possibility he could be negative to the city's efforts for federal grants and other forms of assistance. Maybe not. He was negative toward ethanol, which he didn't seem to be interested in discussing.

I asked for another meeting to which he reluctantly agreed. I travelled to his Washington office. I'd also set meetings with Senator Dan Quayle and senior Senator Richard Lugar.

The meeting with Hiler was very uneasy. The underlying confrontational nature of our first meeting continued. He now made it very clear he was not in favor of ethanol, and that he would not support the ethanol plant for South Bend. It was another short meeting.

His lack of support for the ethanol plant – though a major economic development project in his district – was something I had expected. Nevertheless, I had harbored a small hope he'd be willing to help. I was disappointed.

****

Senator Richard Lugar Takes the Lead

The meeting with Senator Lugar was informal and welcoming. The Senator, former mayor of Indianapolis, understood the challenges facing South Bend which he knew well.

We had a small joke at my expense, but without my

prompting, he readily agreed to take the lead on the ethanol plant for South Bend. He said he supported the development of the ethanol industry and didn't have to be educated on its value for energy independence and the farmers of Indiana.

He promised to work with us for the loan guarantee and everything else needed at the federal level. His support made it easier to gain the backing of Indiana's Republican governor and legislature, something I was concerned about.

Mitchell E. Daniels, then Lugar's chief of staff, (current President of Purdue University) was immensely helpful in moving the required actions through the Senate and U.S. government agencies. And we got to work on all the actions required of the city, county and state governing entities.

Ground Breaking
and Political Controversy

B arry Direnfeld, president of New Energy, asked me to
send out the invitations for the groundbreaking. That
seemed strange at the time. Normally the owners send
out the invitations, but I was happy to do this. Ground breaking was a public event, so my key task was to determine who
should be on the dais and who should be allowed to make
comments.

It didn't take me long to realize why Barry had asked
me to extend the invitations. Turns out that Congressman
Floyd Fithian (D), who was running for the Senate against
Richard Lugar, had called Barry to insist that he be invited to
sit on the dais and to make comments at the groundbreaking.

Congressman Floyd Fithian supported the development of the ethanol industry and was well qualified to be a
U.S. Senator. Under normal circumstances, I would likely
have supported him against Senator Lugar, but these were not
normal circumstances. Senator Lugar had rescued the ethanol plant for South Bend and there was no way I would give

Fithian equal billing to Lugar on the dais. I told Fithian he was welcome to attend the public event, but that's not what he wanted.

Intense political pressure was put on me to invite him to be on the dais and to make comments at the groundbreaking. I was pressured by the chairpersons of the city, county, state, and national Democratic Party to officially invite him. At a local house party for Democrats, Fithian berated me in a confrontation so embarrassing for the hosts and everyone there, that I left to diffuse the situation.

I did not invite Democrat Fithian, nor did I invite Republican Congressman Hiler who had defeated my good friend Congressman Brademas. After the groundbreaking, Senator Lugar's staff told me they appreciated my not bending to the pressure they knew I was under to invite his opponent. Senator Lugar remained a strong friend of South Bend throughout his decades of excellent service in the U.S. Senate.

Groundbreaking for the ethanol plant was a big deal for New Energy and South Bend. And it was a most satisfying accomplishment for me and my staff. More importantly it sent a clear message to the citizenry and the business community that we would pull out all the stops for economic development and matters of importance to South Bend. We would not give up in the face of almost insurmountable odds.

Now it was time for New Energy to build the plant.

Plant Dedication
and Offensive Odor

The sun was bright, the air was pure and it was a mild day in South Bend on October 24, 1984, almost five years after Barry and Don approached me with their plans for an ethanol plant. The dedication was a grand community event with dinners and parties. Indiana Governor Robert D. Orr, Senators Lugar and Quayle, even Senate Majority Leader Howard Baker were on the dais in front of many local dignitaries.

A newspaper reporter wrote that the plant had transformed South Bend into a high synthetic fuel industry, or as he added, "maybe it's just adaptation of the old moonshiner's art of changing corn into alcohol." He was prescient in the sense of the odor caused by old moonshining operations.

When the giant plant cranked up a few days later, a sweet smelling odor, like bread baking or beer brewing, wafted over the southwest side of South Bend, and when the wind picked up, it drifted over a large area of South Bend.

Eight days after the dedication, a fire storm of criticism blew up. People wrote letters to the Tribune that the odor – they called it "stench" – was injurious to their health. They were "personally allergic" to the odor or thought it was "toxic" for everyone. A few thought it might deter business from moving to South Bend and the plant should be shut down. A Tribune editorial called for immediate action, and a group of citizens, named CEASE (Committee of Environmentalists Against the Stench of Ethanol) sued the city and New Energy. What was a grand and joyous event had quickly turned into a public relations disaster.

When we said the odor was worse during startup, it didn't make any difference. When we said city staff had travelled to communities where ethanol was being produced and no one had expressed concerns about odors, it didn't make any difference.

The odor didn't bother me. I had lived in farm country, had taken care of our chickens, fed our pig and milked our cow. But this wasn't about me. I had to do something. I immediately established an odor abatement technical committee and asked the county health officer, Dr. George Plain, to chair it. Dr. Plain had been a very popular physician and an excellent health officer. I was fortunate he accepted the position.

The committee was charged to examine all possible health issues related to the ethanol odor and to recommend ways to abate it. Next we contacted various U.S. federal departments to secure funds that might be needed to purchase the "odor eating" equipment which might be required, and hired a Washington consultant to assist us. This could take millions of dollars which neither the city, nor New Energy had, or so they said.

South Bend was not alone. There were many others who had skin in the ethanol odor situation and felt pressured. The governor, state legislature, our U.S. Senators, the Indiana Air Pollution Control Board, the U.S. Department of Energy, and the Environmental Protection Agency had all supported the plant. They too were pressured to abate the odor. Meanwhile, New Energy was hesitant to discuss its efforts to abate the odor with the technical committee due to the lawsuit filed by CEASE. The City Attorney tried to get CEASE to dismiss their suit, but to no avail.

Regardless, Dr. Plain, city staff and New Energy contacted officials of various state and U.S. departments which led to the U.S. Department of Energy commissioning a chemical analysis of the ethanol plant gases. Involved in this work were the Oak Ridge Laboratories, the Fertilizer Development Center, Muscle Shoals, Alabama, and the Idaho National Engineering Laboratory. Their June 1986 report covered 30 different compounds, and affirmed Dr. Plain's opinion that the odor was harmless and controllable.

Shortly thereafter, the U.S. Department of Energy approved a $3.6 million loan to New Energy to buy and install equipment. On October 1, 1986, the odor eating equipment was selected, which took six months to install. By then, the odor had decreased substantially, but it was still a problem for many.

It had taken two years to get funding and approval for the ethanol plant, two years to build it and two years to fully resolve the odor problem.

By that time, I was well into my second term as mayor. The unique kayak course had been completed in downtown South Bend and we were in the middle of building a highly controversial Class A baseball stadium downtown.

Chapter 8
Who Polluted the Water and More

Catching the Polluter
of Our Drinking Water

April, 1980, 7:00 in the morning. I was in my office preparing a talk to give later that day when I got an urgent, almost panicky phone call from the new and young 28 year old water works director. He said that the water in the Olive Street well field was contaminated with four compounds used as degreasing agents. "Mayor, those are cancer producing compounds. I've shut down all six wells in this field. That's 25 percent of the city's water production. We've got a big problem"

"Thanks for taking quick action. Come to my office and ask the director of public works and the City Attorney to come with you. We have to develop a plan of action and inform the public right away before rumors start about the safety of their water. There's no time to lose."

Our plan was simple in its logic, although complex in its implementation. First, emergency funds would be authorized to increase production of water at the other city wells. Second, consultants would be hired to find the source of the pollutants and to prescribe actions required to reopen the wells. Third, the City Attorney would prepare legal action against the polluter as soon as it was identified – something we were confident we could do, maybe over confident. Fourth, the water works director would immediately call each city council member to inform them of the situation and what actions were being taken.

Immediately after we had fleshed out this plan and council members had been notified, we held a news conference to tell the public that the Olive Street wells had been contaminated, that they were immediately shut down and that their water was safe. These actions satisfied everyone and prevented rumors about unsafe water. Thus we were free to concentrate on remedying the situation.

In December, 1980, just nine months after discovering the contaminants, the source was identified as the Ashland Chemical Company at 1817 West Indiana Avenue, located about 2500 feet from the city's well field. The consultants said that a spill or series of spills, up to 10,000 gallons of contaminated liquid, had occurred about two-and-a half years earlier. Those gallons of contaminated liquid had slowly flowed westward through a vacant lot adjacent to the Ashland property and continued downward to contaminate the city's Olive Street wells.

We immediately notified the Ashland Chemical Company of our findings and began negotiations for payment of damages to the city. This was followed in February, 1981, by a meeting with the federal Environmental Protection Agency (EPA) in Chicago to inform them of the situation and to secure their cooperation. They assured us of their support in solving the matter.

Meanwhile, the city's attorneys were discussing with Ashland's representatives a $1 million plus claim against the firm for polluting the well field. They were told that court litigation would be initiated if Ashland did not voluntarily agree to bear the cost of eliminating the contaminants and putting the wells back in service.

Unfortunately, little progress was made and on May 1, 1981, after many wasteful meetings, we announced that damage claim talks had broken down and we were planning to take Ashland to court. We were determined to fight for the citizens of South Bend and to make the firm pay for its negligence. The city was incurring significant costs and we didn't want to wait years for reimbursement to be made, if at all.

We thought this announcement would be sufficient incentive for Ashland to negotiate seriously with the city, but it didn't work. So to exert more pressure, we informed Ashland it had until August 1, 1981 to agree to a settlement. If it didn't do so, we would file a lawsuit. Ashland did not settle and two days later a $12 million lawsuit was filed against Ashland, demanding $2 million in compensatory damages and $10 million in punitive damages plus court costs.

Filing the lawsuit was a major kick in the pants for the company. Ashland may have believed that the city's legal department and public works staff did not have the knowledge, capability, or guts to sue this large multi-billion-dollar company. They were wrong. (At the time, the city's legal department, small as it was, was arguably the best run law office in South Bend.)

Ashland had a quick change of heart and immediately began serious negotiations. On November 3, 1981, a mere three months after filing the suit and less than a year after the source of the contaminants was identified, we announced an out-of-court settlement with Ashland Oil that was very favorable to our citizens. It included a cash settlement of $640,000 plus thousands of dollars in direct payment to the city's consultants for the removal of contaminated soil on its lot and other areas. Ashland's pollution of the city's Olive Street well field would cost it much in excess of $1 million.

The agreement negotiated by the city with the polluter was hailed by the public for how quickly the city technical staff found the source, and how its legal staff reached a settlement very favorable to the city.

Serving at the Pleasure
of the Mayor

As mayor of South Bend I had the power to remove members of certain boards who served at my pleasure. The word "pleasure" is ironic. It's not likely that removing a member from a board is a pleasure for the board member or the mayor.

Removing a member from such boards is difficult politically and personally. Board members of public entities are usually well-known in the community and are often a friend or political supporter of the mayor. So removing someone who serves at the pleasure of the mayor rarely happens. I knew of no mayor going back many decades who removed a board member serving at his pleasure, except for me.

Most mayoral board appointments cannot be removed by the mayor during their terms. One exception was the South Bend Housing Authority Board of Commissioners whose members serve at the pleasure of the mayor.

I didn't pay much attention to most boards unless they dealt directly with administrative functions of the city such as the Board of Public Safety or the Board of Public Works. However, when things didn't go right with the work of a board to which I appointed members I got involved. Sometimes I was pressured to get involved. This was the case with the South Bend Housing Authority Board of Commissioners.

The Housing Authority was run by a weak executive director who was appointed by the commissioners. He mismanaged the operation, and worse, there were rumors of excessive spending for travel, even misappropriation of funds. Initially, these rumors were not very public and my staff talked with individual commissioners, urging them to take action. Nevertheless nothing happened and eventually these rumors became public. I decided to get personally involved by talking with the commissioners about asking the executive director to resign or to terminate his employment.

No action was taken and the pressure was now on me to terminate the executive director. The problem was that I had no authority to terminate the Housing Authority executive director, something not generally known. However, I did have the authority to ask commissioners to resign or to remove them from the commission, something I was not eager to do. Some were friends, others were political supporters, or both.

There were a variety of reasons why the commissioners did not have the will to fire the executive director. Primarily, it seemed that they could not bring themselves to do so because he was African American. The commission comprised a mix of white and African American members, but the members most opposed to my request were white.

The controversy dragged on in the media and the management of public housing was suffering. Finally, after waiting too long, I removed some of the commissioners and replaced them with persons willing to terminate the executive director.

Personally, I was not too concerned with being

accused of terminating an African American who was not performing as required. To keep anyone in a position who has lost the trust of the community and who cannot do the job properly is not doing the individual and the community a favor.

During all this, I was consulting with a group of African Americans, all friends and political supporters. They were concerned about this issue, knowing that the executive director was hurting the reputation of all African Americans in the community. It's a large and unfortunate problem that if an African American fails to do a good job and is accused of wrong-doing, all African Americans are often placed in the same boat. Hopefully, some day this will not be the case.

My advisors and friends supported my efforts to terminate the executive director, and I fulfilled my promise to them and asked the Housing Authority to appoint an African American as the next executive director, which they did. This person served the Housing Suthority in an exemplary way for decades and received many awards recognizing his outstanding performance.

Taking Election Day Holidays from City Employees Makes No Friends

"Stealing" is what city employees and their unions called taking election day holidays from them.

Something had to give. I thought it was better to take away election day holidays than to reduce city services and freeze employee salaries. In the 1980s, federal funds to cities were being cut and Indiana had imposed stringent controls on the ability of cities to raise taxes for city services. By 1985, cuts would have to be made in essential city services.

I knew taking away election day holidays would be politically tough. It would upset employees and their unions. Democratic Party activists and operatives said this would lead to fewer election-day workers, and would lead to Democrats losing elections – not necessarily in the city which is overwhelmingly Democratic, but for those seeking county, congressional, and higher offices. They predicted it would weaken the Democratic party overall.

That's what I faced as mayor when I proposed a

budget which cut election day holidays to help pay for a modest salary increase. Some people view holidays as an inexpensive way to reward employees. They assume the work gets done anyway. But holidays are very expensive, especially for services which operate 24 hours a day, seven days a week, such as police and fire protection, that cannot be delayed to another day.

Maybe cutting holidays was natural for me. I grew up in a family in a village in a time when the workday was from 7:00 a.m. to 5:00 p.m. with a half hour off for lunch, no breaks, no paid holidays, and no paid vacation. If you didn't work, you didn't get paid. That's the way it was in Acadian French-speaking northern Maine in the 1950s when I started working for money. That's the work ethic I brought to the mayor's office in 1980, maybe that's what brought me to the mayor's office.

However, by then, I had learned that breaks, holidays, and vacations are important to the life of workers and their families, and to work place productivity. But that growing up experience stayed with me. I took few breaks, worked most holidays, and rarely took all my vacation days. Some people called me a workaholic, but it didn't feel that way to me and still doesn't. When work is enjoyable, the negatives of workaholicism don't apply.

I knew from my many political campaigns that the fears of Democratic Party activists and officials were overblown. During the slow demise of political party machines, it had become increasingly difficult to get city workers to work in political campaigns and at the polls on election day. To many city employees, election day holidays were a time to go fishing or to engage in other activities unrelated to elections.

Thankfully, the city council did not give in to the substantial political pressure and voted to take away election day holidays. The sky didn't fall on the Democratic Party.

Election day turnout of voters remained abysmal, but didn't get worse.

Years later, even now, Democratic Party activists – some my friends – blame me, I hope half in jest, for today's uneven performance of the local Democratic Party.

Dealing with a Difficult Councilman: Hire Him to Work for the City?

This councilman was a rough character. He was a gifted mechanic and machinist. He even made bullets for his guns. More than once he demolished a lawyer's argument through a series of well-crafted leading questions, and his comments on issues were on point. He was perhaps the most intelligent person in the council chambers.

But what he had in intelligence, he lacked in emotional stability. He seemed to mask insecurities with a bullying and threatening demeanor. Once he placed a handgun on a table in a small council meeting room to intimidate. He was physically very strong with arms ready to bust out of his shirt sleeves. He drank too much alcohol and worse, he physically abused his wife.

All this was known by many of his constituents, yet they kept him as their councilman. There were politically logical reasons for this. He served his constituents well, pestering – sometimes badgering – city officials privately and publicly to assure ample services for his district. He had become a "man of the people" fighting the establishment.

During my eight years on the city council and as its president, I handled him the best I could. I humored and tolerated him, even when he called me at home half drunk. Still, I respected his talents and often stopped by his mechanics shop to chat about city issues. After I was elected mayor, he became somewhat less confrontational, even more friendly. He bought fishing kits for my two younger children and invited me on his boat in Lake Michigan. But this didn't last.

It wasn't long before he became very difficult, especially after his drinking bouts which happened more and more often. He started calling me in the middle of the night making impossible demands and threatening various sorts of undefined actions. These calls upset my wife and four children . . . and me too. He was also bullying city staff.

In the middle of one night, after I had hung up on him twice, he called again and I lost my cool. I berated him for at least five minutes throwing at him a string of Acadian French cuss words. (Acadian French folks of my day in northern Maine use the sacred items of the Church as swear words, e.g., *hostie* (host), *calice* (chalice), *Jesu, Marie, Joseph* (Jesus, Mary, Joseph). You get the picture. I ended my amateurish attempt to "bully" him by telling him that if he ever called me again in the middle of the night, I would beat him up (not likely since I only weighed 140 pounds to his 225 pounds) and call the police on him (very likely).

He never called me at home again, but he kept bullying the staff. Slowly, maybe too slowly, I came to realize that his presence on the city council was a detriment to South Bend and to himself. He'd become increasingly erratic in his public and private behavior, and I felt something had to be done. But I wasn't sure what to do. Opposing his re-election to the city council was not an option since he was popular in his district.

Eventually, it came to me that if I offered him a city

job and he accepted, he would be legally precluded from serving as councilman. I talked with department directors about this idea which was met with no enthusiasm whatsoever, none wanted him in their department. Nevertheless they agreed something should be done.

Anyway, I decided to approach the councilman with the idea in spite of its potential negative consequences for the administrative staff. It was far from being a perfect solution, but I could think of none better. And it might work. I thought there was a 50/50 chance he would go for it since he seemed to be enjoying his council work less and less.

I went to his garage, packed full of vehicles and heavy machines, for a chat. I told him the city needed his mechanical and machining skills, especially at the wastewater treatment facility in which he had a deep interest. He knew the 50-year-old huge electric motors which required parts that were no longer on the market and had to be individually machined. Plus, he had often complained about the plant's operation. Although we didn't discuss this, he knew about the pension which would come with a city job.

The expression on his face showed surprise. "Let me think about this a bit," he said. He continued working on an engine for a while, maybe five minutes, but it seemed much longer to me. He asked me to give him a nearby wrench. Then without a question, he accepted my offer.

The not-too-happy director of public works worked out the details with him. He was not an easy employee. He gave his supervisors a hard time, but they made it work. They came to value his technical skills and savvy which saved the city tens of thousands of dollars. Over the years he mellowed a bit and was less cantankerous.

Years later, whenever I met him, he gave me a hug and said, "Roger, we sure gave them hell, didn't we." And I said, "We sure did, but you gave them much more hell than I did." He laughed.

"Mayor Can't Win in Bridget Case," or Paying for Mistakes

That was the headline of Jack Colwell's column in the August 19, 1983 South Bend Tribune. I was in the middle of my re-election campaign for a second term as mayor when his column came out. He was right, there was no way I could win in the Bridget case.

Bridget's was a bar with the full name of Bridget McGuire's Filling Station. It was near the University of Notre Dame and had a well-deserved reputation for serving minors. Eventually, Bridget's lost its liquor license and became a coffee house after officers who had raided the place discovered that of 172 patrons in the bar, 165 were under 21. But I'm getting ahead of my story. This was not the issue that got Colwell's attention.

The owners of Bridget's, a powerful state legislator and his sister, were granted a building permit to expand their bar in violation of city zoning that prohibited expansion of a bar based on how close it was to other bars. The neighbors, who followed zoning issues closely, discovered the expansion and complained loudly.

What was I to do? I could ignore the neighbors' pleas and tell them it was a mistake about which I could do nothing since the expansion was half constructed. However, I had built a strong reputation of enforcing zoning and building codes and felt a strong duty to protect the integrity of the zoning ordinance.

I decided in favor of protecting the integrity of the city's zoning ordinance by doing the only thing we could do. I issued a stop order on the construction and mandated demolishing the half-built addition. I knew the neighbors would be happy but I also knew that many persons would question my judgment because it might eventually require the city to pay damages to the owners.

The owners appealed the decision to the Board of Zoning Appeals, which denied their appeal. They threatened to sue the city and me personally for damages unless the city cancelled the stop order and the requirement to demolish. Triple damages they said. The state legislator even alleged that the stress caused by this issue had landed him in the hospital. But I was not going to change my position. We had thought it out carefully and felt deeply that it was important for the integrity of the zoning ordinance to be consistent in its enforcement, even when it might be expensive for the city to do so.

There was pressure on me from many sides, so we proposed a way to resolve the issue without actually demolishing the addition. We told the owners they could finish the construction, if they agreed to not to use it as a bar area. They could use it for storage or some other way.

The state legislator and his sister were not willing to lose out on this and did not accept our offer. I can't blame them. It was the city's fault they were granted a building permit in violation of a city ordinance. However, they were not entirely blameless. They were aware of the zoning ordinance and should have known that their request for a building

145

permit was in violation of the ordinance. We never made that point in public since it would not have helped to resolve the matter.

In another effort to reach an accommodation in a reasonable way, we offered to pay the owners $40,000 to cover their costs of the half constructed addition and allow them to keep the addition, but only for storage. This was an offer I thought they would accept, but they refused and filed suit against the city and me in circuit court. The issue had become a very public one and the owners wanted to have us lose in court and possibly get a larger settlement.

Next came a fortuitous and totally unexpected event. During the interminable legal maneuverings, the owners and their attorney missed a court mandated deadline and they lost their case. The city won by default and did not have to pay any damages. Still, we didn't force the demolition of the half constructed addition and allowed them to keep it for storage.

Meanwhile, before the issue was resolved, the election had taken place and I had won easily. I came out well politically, but my administration's reputation for operating almost flawlessly was damaged a bit.

Jack was right. We didn't win in a situation caused by our bungling, but we didn't lose in court because of the owners' bungling.

Chapter 9
What I Learned on
the School Board

"You're Crazy to
Run for the School Board"

T hat's what my friends said when I told them I was
running for the school board in 2008. And when my
wife said, "Run if you must, but I won't be involved in
this campaign," it gave me pause. I couldn't blame her. She
had been active in my eight political campaigns (city council
and mayor) and that was enough for her. It should have been
enough for me too, but run for the school board I did.

I had become frustrated over the negative reputation
of South Bend schools which had once been the pride of its
citizens and I thought my experience would permit me to
bring our schools to a higher level. I had a master's degree in
education from the University of Notre Dame, had been a
Peace Corps teacher, and my mother plus four of my 9 siblings
had been teachers. Education is in my blood. So is politics,
and there's more of it in education than most people want to
admit.

Superintendents and board members blamed the
schools' poor reputation on many factors: the flight of middle

class parents to suburban schools, inadequate state funding for urban schools, the "nosy" media, disruptive students, parents who do not prepare their children for school, and so on. I didn't accept these reasons for failure even though I knew they were factors in the performance of our schools. My experience told me they were obstacles. I had attended a one-room high school for two years and had taught in Thailand where resources were extremely limited, yet academic achievement was quite good. To me these challenges were obstacles to overcome, not reasons to blame others.

I thought a major cause of the district's negative reputation was the dysfunctional school board. And as I learned after a few years on the school board, it was also the result of dysfunctional administrations. So in 2008, I filed papers with the county clerk for an at-large seat, and adopted the slogan, "World Class Schools for South Bend." I won easily.

My first days on the board were met with skepticism by the other six members whose attitude seemed to be: Does this former mayor think he can do a better job than us? That didn't bother me. My previous political tussles as city council president and mayor had given me a very tough skin. There wasn't much they could do to me that hadn't been done before.

I'm Gonna Start
a New Tech High School

I got to work immediately. I'd promised to work for world class schools which meant large changes in the way schools are structured and how students are taught. When I learned of the New Tech school model being pushed by community leaders, I decided to join them on visits to New Tech high schools in Sacramento, California, and Columbus, Indiana. I was very impressed.

New Tech schools are a dramatic move from the lock-step traditional school based on the old factory model to a more open project-based learning. School floor plans are radically different – classrooms are open, no doors, large inside windows. Students work in groups on projects selected with the teacher who is a guide or coach. There are no bells, students have to be on time for class as they would have to be for work. Accountability is to the teacher and the student group. A nonperforming member can be "fired" from the group.

The New Tech high school model speaks to the problem facing our schools that are constantly subjected to small changes at the margins, but which leave unchanged the heart of the system. This new model hits directly at the heart, so I pushed it hard on the superintendent and the school board immediately upon taking office in January 2009.

There was enthusiastic support for a New Tech high school in the community, but unfortunately, only tepid support from the administration and the board. Public hearings were held, questions were answered, but that wasn't enough to gain board and staff support. In August 2009, the New Tech proposal was soundly defeated.

I promised right then and there that I would help start a charter New Tech high school. Board members were incredulous and the administrative staff was shocked. They and many others couldn't believe that a public school board member would establish a charter school. Controversy erupted, but I didn't care. The system needed the major changes represented by the New Tech model.

I organized a diverse and talented board of directors, incorporated New Schools, Inc. as a nonprofit, raised funds, hired a consultant, and consulted with Ball State University and the State Board of Education who supported our efforts. We were fast on the way to getting a New Tech high school established. To express our unflagging support for public schools, we told the school board that after the New Tech was fully established, in about four years, we would give it to the school corporation.

Initially, the board and superintendent had not believed I could get this done. They probably thought I was bluffing. But when they realized I was well on the way to success, they reversed themselves and decided to establish their own New Tech high school. I was surprised but happy to vote for it. That's what I had pushed for in August, 2009 but had lost. Later we, New Schools, Inc., suspended our efforts and offered to help the school corporation establish its New Tech school.

My Vote is Not Enough

The board's New Tech negative vote and reversal after my year-long effort to start a charter New Tech convinced me that my single vote would be woefully inadequate to move toward world class schools. I would need a majority. After the negative vote I began planning to defeat three of the board members who had voted against the New Tech model and who were up for re-election in 2010.

I was even more convinced of the need to elect new school board members after learning through meetings with school board members, administrators, principals, and teachers of a very unhealthy, indeed, a poisoned relationship between some board members and the school administration.

Some board members had used their position to "force" the hiring and promotion of family members and friends in the school district. Superintendents were probably happy to comply with the requests, thus gaining leverage over the board. A favor for a board member likely obliged that member to return the favor, or face the possibility of retaliation against an employee who was a relative or friend. This conflicted relationship gave excessive influence to the superintendent over the board and directly affected the board's ability to provide objective oversight to the administration.

I intensified my efforts to defeat the three school board members. Two persons had announced their intention to oppose two members and I convinced a friend to run against the third. I raised funds, worked for their election, and they won. I should add that they won because they were well qualified candidates who had campaigned effectively.

On January 1, 2011, three new school board members provided a majority for serious change in our schools and I was elected president. I convinced the board we needed a new superintendent and they asked me to convey that message to him. When I told him the board wanted a change of direction, he retired. We began the search for a new superintendent. My hopes were high.

How Not to
Recruit a Superintendent

We had done everything right. We had hired a highly recommended executive recruitment group whose specialty was school administrators. We had followed a comprehensive and transparent process that had involved citizens in identifying the characteristics of highly qualified candidates. And we had asked for the inclusion of non-traditional candidates who had excelled in either business, non-profits, or government, not only those with educational administration experience.

After a long process the recruitment group recommended three candidates to interview. I was disappointed that none came from the non-traditional sector. All had extensive experience in educational administration. One candidate was a person we had retained earlier to be interim superintendent.

We were not satisfied with the results of the search, but we had no choice but to move on. We set appointments for the candidates to meet with the public and for private interviews with the board. We hoped one would meet our requirements.

Bad news. Before any of the interviews, a reporter had Googled the candidates and had quickly discovered that one of them had a flawed public record that would never pass our integrity test. No need to say more except there was no point even letting him come for the already scheduled interview. I disinvited the candidate amidst controversy. He was the only African American candidate, and a few members of the board and some citizens felt he should be interviewed. I resisted those efforts.

Our search had received rave reviews for its thoroughness and openness, but now it could fast devolve into a circus due to our consultants not doing even cursory background checks of the candidates. I was concerned and moved quickly. After a brief discussion about re-opening the search, we decided to interview the two remaining candidates

Neither candidate met our full requirements, but the interim superintendent seemed to be open to the kinds of changes we desired in our schools. I was skeptical about her, but a majority of the board felt there was nothing else we could do at that point. We gave her a three-year contract, hoping that with the leadership of the board, she would be able to lead South Bend schools to a higher level.

We had done our job. But the highly recommended consultants had not aggressively sought non-traditional candidates, had recommended less than stellar individuals from the educational sector, and had not vetted them adequately. They had not done their job.

I didn't know then that executive recruiting groups who are focused on educational leaders and managers tend to have a narrow perspective. They generally come from the educational sector and too often believe that the best qualified superintendents come from that sector. Plus, such consulting groups accumulate a "stable" of educators seeking superintendent positions which likely makes them conflicted.

It would have been more productive to retain consultants with experience recruiting top executives for business, nonprofit, and government. They would likely have had a better chance of finding candidates who better understood the educational requirements of our modern economy. I'm still disappointed today about our search for a new superintendent.

Paying the Price
for Censuring an Elected
School Board Member

What do you do with an elected school board member who repeatedly ignored state laws and the school board bylaws?

He had become a "darling" of the media by feeding them confidential information from executive sessions on personnel and other legally protected matters. He had publicly impugned the integrity of board members and staff, and disrupted the proceedings of the board. Some board members and school administrators were fearful of his threatening demeanor. He was a bully.

As president of the school board, I had made numerous private appeals for him to stop, but these hadn't worked. Something had to be done. Unfortunately, there were few options. Removing him from the board wasn't practical since it's extremely difficult to take out an elected official from any legislative body. So the vice president and I decided to ask board members to publicly censure him. A school board censuring one of its members had never been done in South

Bend, maybe not anywhere in Indiana.

The process was long and contentious. His supporters championed and defended him. So did the media. The South Bend Tribune editorialized on the matter, calling it at one point an ugly issue. Finally the vote was taken and he was censured 4 to 2 with one abstention. (Nothing irritates me more than a member of a legislative body who doesn't have the guts to take a difficult vote.)

All this was happening in the year that the censured board member and I were running for re-election. Some people thought the move to censure had been intended to make him lose his re-election bid. This was not my motive, although I would not have been unhappy if he had lost. As it turned out he won re-election by a small margin, and I won easily. Many people were convinced that his public censure by the board had galvanized his supporters. It probably did.

I don't understand (maybe I don't want to understand) why citizens who would not tolerate disruptive and improper behavior by someone serving on their company board, or a symphony board, seem willing to tolerate that kind of behavior by a member of a legislative body doing the public's business.

Maybe appointing an independent citizen group to advise the board on this type of issue would be more effective. Yet it would be difficult to find citizens willing to serve on such a committee. Disciplining anyone is a distasteful process. Doing so publicly is even more so. Furthermore, citizens groups are not necessarily immune from partisan political pressure. They can and do get involved in political shenanigans. And after such group had given its advice, the responsibility would still be the board's.

During my days as mayor I had appointed a citizens group to recommend three candidates for an important policy making group from which I would select one. The citizens group played more politics with their deliberations and recommendations than I would have done. Of the three persons they recommended to me, two were patently unqualified, "forcing" me to appoint their choice. I became very wary of asking citizens groups to make such recommendations to me after that. Advice, yes. Recommendations, no.

Looking back, I doubt I would try to censure an elected member of a legislative body again. I think I ended up being "censured" by the public more than the censured board member.

How Not to Be
a School Superintendent

The interim superintendent became the new superintendent in October, 2011. The first thing she did was to bring some of her cronies from previous positions to work for her and to move administrative people around. It felt like rearranging the deck chairs on the Titanic. I opposed much of this, but other members wanted to give her the staff she wanted.

Even more galling was the lack of attention and support for the New Tech high school which had been grudgingly approved by the board and the previous superintendent. It was only given lip service. A few years after I left the school board, she "rebranded" and merged it with some other programs. The South Bend School district may well be the only place in the country that tried to establish a New Tech high school and failed.

This and much more led to my resignation from the board. Under her leadership, the 2.0 GPA adopted by the school board, which was required for students to participate in extracurricular activities, was first ignored, then gutted.

My suggestion that some principals be sent to a high-powered training program for six months was met with the retort that the district staff could provide such training in-house.

The new superintendent was not interested in new school models, such as a teacher-run school, which some teachers were eager to try, or contracting with successful organizations to run our failing schools, such as those who administer Green Dot Schools and Kipp Schools.

The new superintendent and her staff were concentrated on what had become very comfortable to them over the years. Toying around with the curriculum and reorganizing the administrative setup, they were eager to do, but changing the basic schooling system, they were not.

The large question facing our school board and educators is how to move the South Bend school system away from an old factory regimented model to one based on the new, flexible and fast moving economy. This superintendent, in spite of a board open to major changes, was not going to lead the way.

Knowing when to leave a position is important. I had done what I could for five-and-one- half years on the board. It was time to move on, and I resigned.

School Boards Are
Not the Problem

During my five and one-half-years on the school board, I learned that school boards are not the primary stumbling block to the creation of world-class school systems. The critical problem is the paucity of top educational administrators, particularly superintendents. Most do not have the training and leadership experience equal to the challenges facing public school.

One reason for the lack of world class leaders in public school districts comes from the preparation superintendents receive in universities. Many of their university professors and instructors moved "up" from secondary and elementary school. There's strength in that, but there's also weakness. This can result in the recycling of the same knowledge and practices over and over again with little input from other disciplines and from the consumers of school services.

Also, superintendents and other school administrators seem averse to the personal and professional risks involved in initiating system change. And sometimes they appear unwilling or unable to partner with parents, business, and the community in constructive ways.

Given the lack of top flight educational leaders, it's imperative that school boards aiming to transform their school districts look for exceptional leaders in areas such as the business community, nonprofit organizations, and government, not only among typically trained educators.

School boards, no matter how well-intentioned and competent, are limited in what they can do to initiate major changes. A board monitors, prods, and evaluates the superintendent, but unless the board has retained a world class superintendent, the district will not reach world class status. And once a superintendent is hired, the die is cast for the typical three-year contract, unless one wants to go through superintendents every few years, not a good idea.

This brings me back to the challenge of finding and appointing a superintendent open to new ways of preparing students for an economy based on disruption, fast change, new jobs requiring new skills, indeed a different kind of economy and world.

Chapter 10
Getting Things Done
in the Peace Corps

Sarge says, "You Volunteers Are Creating the Peace Corps"

"It's you volunteers who are creating the Peace Corps, not us in Washington," said Sargent Shriver, first director of the Peace Corps. He was visiting my school in Udorn, Thailand in 1962 where I was teaching carpentry.

I had written to President Kennedy in February 1961, "If you are going to establish the Peace Corps, I would like to serve in it." And just months after the President established the Peace Corps by executive order on March 1, 1961, I had received a telegram from Sargent Shriver to report for training at the University of Michigan. On my 23rd birthday in January, 1962, I arrived in Bangkok eager to get to :work in Northeast Thailand – its poorest area.

I thought "Sarge" (that's what we called him) was putting me on. I didn't feel I was helping to create the Peace Corps. I was just out to help poor people in a poor country and to have an adventure. But reflecting on that time has made me realize the essential role of the early volunteers in creating the Peace Corps.

It's easy to forget that in 1961, President Kennedy's idea of people-to-people diplomacy ~ of sending young (and not so young) Americans to help people in poor countries – was one which had many skeptics. Numerous diplomats and prominent persons, even the late President Dwight D. Eisenhower, had predicted its failure.

However, the tens of thousands who had volunteered for the Peace Corps even before it was established was a robust antidote to the skepticism. Still, numbers and enthusiasm would not be enough. The Peace Corps idea would have to be implemented in the field by the volunteers, each with their own idea of what would make an effective volunteer.

I was not sure how I would approach being a Peace Corps Volunteer, but I was full of confidence that I had the needed attributes and skills to be effective. I was naïve, but naïveté can be a powerful force as long as it's leavened with the willingness to learn and a little bit of humility. Willingness to learn I had, sufficient humility, not so sure.

On the flight from Presque Isle, Maine, to the University of Michigan for training, I imagined myself in a small village, living with a Thai family, teaching carpentry, learning to speak Thai and experiencing the people and their culture. Those were the ideas I started with and that were emphasized during training. We were told we were not there to impose our way of life, but to learn and respect the Thai culture. Flexibility and adaptability were stressed at every opportunity. In Thailand we would be on our own with very little supervision from the small and equally inexperienced Bangkok staff. That was okay with me since I didn't want any supervision. My view was, send me my monthly stipend and I'll be fine.

Upon arrival at my school in Udorn, my adaptability was immediately tested. I quickly learned that the school did not need a carpentry teacher. So I met with the school director (principal) and discussed modifying my assignment, which he was very willing to do. He had probably not been consulted by his supervisors in Bangkok about having a volunteer at his school, nor had the Peace Corps been in direct contact with him. This has changed in today's Peace Corps, but adaptability of the volunteer is still very much required.

We re-worked my assignment to work in the school library, teach English and some mathematics involved in carpentry such as figuring the pitch of a roof. I also added the Girls Handicraft School to my assignment, where I taught English occasionally.

These and other decisions helped me to become the volunteer I had imagined. I made mistakes, learned to listen to my colleagues at the school, and to be more humble. I and the first volunteers in Thailand and in other countries helped determine the approach, philosophy and public image of the Peace Corps for years to come. I guess Sarge was right. We volunteers were creating the Peace Corps.

Becoming the Peace Corps Volunteer I Wanted to Be

When I arrived in Udorn, Thailand, with my colleagues, we were provided a comfortable traditional Thai house on the Teacher Training College campus. My colleagues were assigned to the Teacher Training College, and I was assigned to the Udorn Trade School. The house was made of teakwood, built on stilts about 10 feet off the ground. It had three bedrooms, a western-style toilet and shower, a small kitchen, and a living room with one wall of doors which opened to a large veranda that overlooked the campus. It was a great place to relax and speak English after a full day of teaching in a language still foreign to us.

I loved our house, our neighbors, and our camaraderie; I was comfortable. Yet, I was uneasy and dissatisfied with my situation: I was not learning to speak Thai and the local dialect quickly enough, and I was not getting to know my Thai colleagues at the Trade School, where I taught carpentry and English, except on a superficial level. The Trade School occupied a lower social status than the Teacher Training College, and so did its teachers. My residence at the college widened the social gap between my colleagues and me, and made it more difficult to bridge. I was happy and enjoyed living in Thailand, but I was not living up to my idea of a Peace Corps Volunteer.

I asked Pricha, my principal, if I could have a room in a house owned by the Trade School. He didn't like the idea, saying the house was too old and would not be good enough for me. He thought I would miss living with my Peace Corps friends, have a hard time using the squat toilets, and would dislike "showering" by splashing water on myself from a large jar while wrapped in a pawkama (a sarong type cloth for men, tied at the waist) for privacy. Principal Pricha had studied for some months at the University of Hawaii; he knew the comfortable American lifestyle, and he understood our greater need and desire for personal privacy.

I persisted. I explained to Principal Pricha that living with a Thai family would help me learn the language, the culture, and family life more than was possible living with my two American buddies at the Teacher Training College. This final argument won him over and he relented. He arranged for me to live in a house next door to the school with Charoon and Luk (Not their real names) teachers at the Trade School, and their two young families. Deep down, I think he was very pleased to have his Peace Corps Volunteer living near the school and becoming a more intimate part of his school family.

My new home was a simple and large rambling structure, built with teakwood that had darkened with age inside and outside, giving the house a somber, almost haunting look, particularly at night. It was built on stilts about five or six feet off the ground - a necessity since the house lay nearly three feet below the grade of the road, a couple hundred feet away. When a big rain fell, water would run off the road, down the lot, under and around our house, forming a pond behind it, where the family would fish. I'm still not sure how fish happened in a pond formed by rain where no pond existed most of the year. According to the people in my house, it just happened.

Windows were simple openings with no glass or screens, but there were wooden shutters hung from the inside, for privacy. Screens were installed in my room to keep out the mosquitoes and the bugs. To Thai people, screens were a western thing, and they didn't want any for themselves. They also provided me with a regular western-style bed and mosquito netting – the mosquitoes made their way to my room despite the screen in the window.

The sitting areas, kitchen, and toilet facilities were common to all. Each family had a large room for sleeping and other private uses, and I had a small bedroom for the same purposes. In addition to my western-style bed, my room had an armoire, a desk with a lamp, and more private space than I had in my Lille home where I grew up with nine brothers and sisters. This large house was covered by a very old and very rusty tin roof which amplified the noise of rain to a thunderous roar.

Adjusting to the squat-type toilets was easy, and bathing in the open by splashing water from a huge jar, while struggling to keep the pawkama from falling off, soon became second nature. There was no western-style shower in the house because of no running water in the house. The water needed to drink, cook, clean house, and wash our bodies came from captured rain or was carried in buckets from sources some distance away. Adjusting to the two families and having little privacy was not a problem for someone raised with nine siblings.

Living with Charoon's and Luk's families and their children was the best decision I made as a volunteer. I quickly became more proficient in Thai and the local dialect - spoken in our home almost always. I got a first-hand education in

Thai family life, how they cared for children and how they related to each other and their extended family members. I also developed closer and deeper relationships with my colleagues at the Trade School.

Peace Corps
and Politics in Haiti

Four days after leaving the mayor's office on January 1,
1988, I was directing the Peace Corps in Haiti. Reverend Theodore Hesburgh C.S.C., President of Notre
Dame, had introduced me to Peace Corps Director Loret
Miller Ruppe who had suggested I run the program in Haiti. I
accepted.

It was a chaotic time in Haiti. Even before my arrival,
all Peace Corps volunteers had been evacuated for their safety.
Still, when given the choice of waiting to leave until things
settled down, I had refused. I was eager to bring the volunteers back to Haiti. My family would join me after school let
out in June.

Haiti was in the middle of a dechoucage (uprooting)
of the Ton Ton Macoute - the feared private goon squad of
deceased Papa Doc (Francois Duvalier) and of his son, Baby
Doc (Jean Claude). Citizens were still being terrorized by
the Macoutes and the political situation was highly unstable
with the government controlled by the military. I would be
learning a new politics.

My priority was to assess the security of volunteers' worksites, all outside Port-au-Prince, (PAP) the capital city. However the American embassy had prohibited travel outside PAP, making it extremely difficult for me to assess security. I could not depend just on the briefings of embassy personnel since most of them, even in normal times, tended to rely on second-hand information. I needed first-hand knowledge.

Luckily, one of the first persons I met in Haiti was the embassy's military attaché, Major Robert Goyette. He knew more about security in Haiti than anyone else. He did not seem burdened by the travel prohibition, visited throughout Haiti, and he knew the generals running the country. Plus, we had a similar French language / cultural background, and we became good friends. His advice and support enhanced my understanding of security issues in critical ways.

I approached my work in Haiti like I did as mayor in South Bend. I depended on an excellent staff and reached out to people outside official circles for advice and support. I met with the director of the Pan American Development Foundation who had lived in Haiti for decades, and the director of Catholic Relief Services. They knew Haiti well and provided invaluable advice on security.

In spite of the travel prohibition, and after I had sufficiently learned the lay of the land, I visited volunteers' sites and talked with the staffs of their host organizations. To supplement my information, I decided to visit the mayor of Port-au-Prince. I didn't think this was a big deal, but the Haitian staff was against this idea, saying he was a dangerous man, had killed many people, and was part of the Macoutes.

I went anyway. I thought visiting him would help develop a personal relationship with an important official and give me a different slant on security. I didn't tell the ambassador about this since he would have immediately nixed the idea. I had learned long ago from an old Holy Cross priest not to ask for permission. "Just do what you think should be done," he had said.

City hall was a fortress. There were Macoutes all over, brandishing their Uzis – easy to recognize by their swagger and dark glasses. They inspected the undercarriage of my vehicle with mirrors, opened the trunk, and checked my identification. They patrolled at the entrance, walked the hallway, and stood by his door. I was not intimidated . . . maybe I should have been.

The mayor not only spoke his native creole, he knew French, English, and some Spanish. "Use any language," he said. But after a few pleasantries in French, he switched to English. I think he wanted to show me how well he spoke it. We talked about our children – we both had two in U.S. colleges, one of his was studying to be a physician.

We discussed security, and he stressed that I shouldn't worry at all about security. "We don't attack Americans," he said, "we love Americans." His was not the last word on security for volunteers, but he was correct. At the time, Haitians did not attack Americans.

Unfortunately, the political and security situation did not improve enough to bring back the volunteers in my first year. During 1988 there were four coups, one headed by the general who lived across the street from me. (Grenades exploded in the street and I could hear shots from Uzis blasting away. It scared my two teenage daughters who were with me at the time). The Peace Corps correctly decided to suspend operations for the time being.

I was asked to direct the Peace Corps in the Eastern Caribbean (from Grenada) and to be available to restart the program in Haiti. In 1989, Haiti settled down enough to reopen the program. I commuted between Grenada and Haiti every two weeks, a two day jaunt since I had to get there by way of Miami. It was very rewarding to bring the volunteers back to Haiti, the poorest country in the Americas.

This was not an easy time for my family, but it had

provided a unique and unforgettable experience. We saw extreme poverty and violence first-hand. One day in Grenada, my 11-year-old son said, "Dad, most people in the world are poor aren't they?"

"Get Those Two Peace Corps Volunteers Out of My City"

The deputy mayor of Varna, Bulgaria's third largest city, said, "If you don't get those two Peace Corps Volunteers out of Varna, we'll kick them out." This was 1994, and I was the Peace Corps director in Bulgaria.

I love the Peace Corps. I had volunteered in 1961 even before it was officially established. In 1988 I rejoined as director of the Peace Corps in Haiti and in 1993, I was named Peace Corps director in Bulgaria.

It was no coincidence that the deputy mayor had called me since I had met with him and the Mayor of Varna earlier. As a former mayor, I always enjoyed sharing stories with other mayors, and they did too. Plus, there were volunteers in Varna, and it was good public relations to call on the mayor where we had volunteers.

The deputy's call was about two volunteers who had apparently become quite troublesome. The volunteers had threatened to stop a grant for the city library unless they were appointed to the board. They had helped secure that grant and now they were using it to force themselves on the board.

The mayor was not having any of this and wanted them out of Varna. He remembered me – he had probably not met too many mayors of U.S. cities – and he had asked his deputy to call me about it. He wanted to handle the problem as diplomatically as possible. He knew the Peace Corps was a popular American program and he wanted to maintain a cordial relationship with the American Embassy.

I was appalled at the behavior of those two volunteers and told the deputy mayor that the volunteers' demand was entirely inappropriate and against Peace Corps policy. I didn't add that their behavior was naïve and culturally insensitive because I didn't want to unduly detract from the Peace Corps reputation. I told the deputy I would handle this promptly and asked him for a few weeks' time. He agreed and thanked me.

The very next day I boarded an old Soviet-era two-propeller plane to Varna and met with the two volunteers. I raked them over the coals, ignored their excuses, ordered them to pack their bags, and leave for Sophia immediately. They were flabbergasted and couldn't understand what they had done wrong, one indication that the Peace Corps volunteer selection and training process had failed them and the Peace Corps.

I met with the deputy mayor and told him the volunteers were leaving that day and would not return to Varna, thus resolving a small diplomatic tangle. In gratefulness, he took me to a great Bulgarian restaurant for lunch. This is one of my pleasant memories of a Bulgaria recently freed from its stifling relationship with the Soviet Union, and whose citizens were still highly suspicious of each other and foreigners.

Chapter 11
Creating World
Dignity, Inc.

Tsunami Hits
Khao Lak, Thailand

On December 26, 2004, a 33-foot-tall tsunami hit Khao Lak, pushing a navy boat almost two miles inland, killing thousands of tourists, workers and residents. I wanted to help, so when the Peace Corps called for volunteers, I said yes.

By May 2005, I was in Khao Lak, a small town where homes, hotels, resorts, and other businesses had been destroyed. Survivors had no jobs no income, bodies were still being discovered, and funerals were a daily occurrence. Sadness permeated the community. You could see it in people's faces and feel it. Visiting a village hit hard by the tsunami made me tear up when a grandmother, tears running down her face, told me of her four grandchildren who had perished in the tsunami.

I was assigned to the Tsunami Volunteer Center, established by a Thai foundation to welcome volunteers from all over the world and to put them to work. Volunteers were assigned to build homes, fishing boats, simple furniture and general cleanup. They also developed programs for children whose schools had been demolished.

The center's director had been told I was a former mayor and he wasn't sure what to do with me because being mayor is a big deal in Thailand, not so much for me. Knowing this, I told the director I would do anything, clean restrooms, do paper work, answer the phones. Whatever.

They didn't ask me to clean toilets, but it was a volunteer task and I pitched in. I did paper work, interviewed volunteers, and anything else. Soon though, the director asked me to direct the day-to-day operations of the center. He felt the center would benefit from my management experience and knowledge of the Thai language and culture – many volunteers were Thai. My knowing French would be useful with volunteers from places like the Netherlands, Switzerland, France, and Canada.

Most volunteers from outside Thailand knew little or nothing about Thai culture so I developed a one-day orientation on how to get things done in Thailand, and about the center's approach. We were to respect the culture, experience, and dignity of those whose lives had been destroyed by the tsunami. They were desperate, had lost sons, daughters, homes, and jobs, and had to accept charity, but we wanted to do this in way to enhance their dignity and self-respect.

We worked hand-in-hand with the victims. We solicited their advice on designing what would be their homes, furniture, and fishing boats. We asked for their labor and skills, which they were very eager to give. In this way, we respected them and hopefully furthered their dignity. Each home and fishing boat had the personal touch of the people building it.

The center's approach was a powerful contrast to that of other organizations that had flocked to help those affected by the tsunami. I don't want to denigrate them all, but some were blissfully unaware of the need to respect the people's culture and dignity. One Christian-based organization seemed more interested in recruiting converts than in helping. It even required recipients of their aid to attend their church services.

My six-month commitment was fast coming to an end, the need for volunteers was ebbing, and the Tsunami Volunteer Center would soon close. I would be leaving, but there were long term needs in education and other areas that I wanted to carry on. So did another former Peace Corps Volunteer and his Thai wife, David and Bui Rubin. We had become friends while they had been volunteering and using their personal funds to buy and transport food for the children's educational programs.

We talked about continuing our work, and decided on a nonprofit organization. He and his wife would direct the work in Thailand where they lived half the year.

By January 2006, my wife, Rolande, and I had incorporated World Dignity, Inc., and with seed money from board members we began. Next: The work of World Dignity, Inc.

World Dignity, Inc.: Principles and Philosophy

World Dignity, Inc. (WDI) is a different helping organization. We're small and flexible, allowing us to respond effectively and creatively to the challenges facing economically poor people. It is volunteer-run, with very low overhead, allowing most of the donations to be directed to the people we serve.

We listen to the people we work with, devise programs based on their culture and needs, and require their financial and work participation. Preserving the dignity of those we assist and that of our donors is a high priority.

Our focus is on the education of students in Thailand, South India, Bangladesh, and South Bend. I list our guidelines below and hope to bring these to life in the next pages.

1. Work with poor people only at their invitation.
2. Develop and shape programs with the people to be affected by them.
3. Respect the culture / ways of operating.

4. Work in areas we know well, or can get to know well.
5. Consider the long term effects and sustainability of our activities.
6. Enhance the dignity of the people affected by the programs and activities.
7. Require the volunteer and financial participation of program beneficiaries.
8. Make the highest and best use of volunteers.
9. Serve poor people of any race, national origin, sexual, religious, or political orientation.
10. Evaluate programs and activities periodically.

Smart Kids in South Bend

Smart Kids was an after-school program for students who were academically failing in the fifth and sixth grades, but it was not a program to catch up on school work. I felt that since the students were failing in the classroom, I should try a different method.

A friend and I met twice a week with five or six students 90 minutes each day. Basic to our approach was that we included the students in planning each session. The students loved this, and when we forgot one time, they reminded us – not surprising since everything else during the school day was planned for them.

Our motto, pasted to the wall, was: Everyone is Smart at Something. We recited this at the start of every session. At first, a few school staff thought it presumptuous to call students who were failing academically, smart kids. But soon, the students called themselves smart kids.

Another maxim was: Reading + Service = Dignity + Self-Respect. I had asked the principal to give us chores in the school and he had done so. Service was incorporated in each session, something the Smart Kids looked forward to. I knew that in some cultures students clean their classrooms, and research shows that students involved in service to their school and community do better academically.

We treated the Smart Kids as smart kids. Every session included reading poems such as Wordsworth's "To The Cuckoo," Japanese haikus, folk tales like "Catching a Thief," and African sayings like "Your freedom is in your head." The students loved those poems.

During one session, a student said he wanted to design a school, so we sent him up to the blackboard. He quickly drew a classroom with windows looking out into the hallway, something modern schools are doing to mimic the open nature of today's work place. Then he drew a toilet enclosed down to the floor to prevent kids from looking up in it. (Who would have thought?)   The Smart Kids had smarts not measured in the traditional classroom setting which, disastrously, pegged them "slow" or even worse, "dumb."

My experience with the Smart Kids program had convinced me to run for the school board which, unfortunately, led me to drop my involvement in the Smart Kids program. Some people felt that a board member running a program in one school showed favoritism.

Still, I miss this experience.

Phi Sohn Nong and
Work and Study

When we asked the principals of schools on Koh Yao Yai and Lek (big and small islands off the coast of southern Thailand) about their concerns, they said that poor students often dropped out of school because they did not have money to pay for transportation, books and fees. We wanted to help, but didn't want to just give money to the students.

After many conversations, we agreed that World Dignity would provide funds to pay the students a small stipend for work in their school. The school would create the jobs, select the students, set up a special bank account to receive the funds and administer the program pro bono. This would not be charity.

Initially, the jobs were to clean rooms, work in the library, or in the school yard and so on. But rather quickly, without our involvement, the schools added the job of tutoring, asking the more advanced students to tutor the slower ones. We were thrilled. Some of the tutors enjoyed teaching so much they decided to become teachers, and we awarded them Dignity Scholarships to attend college. Now some of these former tutors are teaching in their former schools.

The school staffs had taken over the program, made it into something much better than we could have done on our own. This experience reaffirmed what happens when the people who need assistance are asked what would work best, based on their needs, culture and abilities, instead of being offered a cookie-cutter program as is often the case.

Give Them Bricks
and They'll Build It

Aself-help Women's Club, organized by the Auroville
Village Action Group in South India, had no place to
meet but in the mud when it rained and in the dust
when it was dry. They asked World Dignity to provide funds
for the bricks and mortar to build a meeting place.

We did not usually provide funds to build anything.
We're focused on educational programs and activities. But
we're small, flexible, and open to people working to lift themselves by their bootstraps. So I asked for a detailed proposal.

The Women's Club is an organization centered on
discussing and acting on the problems in their villages. Their
goals are to enrich their lives and their villages through education, training, and job development. I was impressed. This
was a self-help program, not a hand-out. Plus, they concentrated on education and training, our main interest.

We decided to fund the building materials. The village would provide the labor, thus meeting our requirement
that the beneficiaries contribute to the project. Our dona-

tion was less than a few thousand dollars.

Some months later I received pictures from the club that showed the women building the brick walls, the floor, the roof, and the entire center. I thought the men in the village would be helping, but I was not surprised: it was a women's project. There's a saying that "if you want to get something done in a poor village, work with the women."

A year or so later, Rolande and I, at the invitation of the Women's Club, were talking with about 30 women sitting comfortably in their meeting room. They thanked us too profusely for our help. We had done through World Dignity what we're on earth to do – help one another.

They talked a lot about the challenges facing their villages and themselves, especially those faced by their children. When Rolande asked about their most important needs and desires, a grandmother said, "I would like my granddaughter to get a college education." Without a moment's hesitation, Rolande promised we would make that happen.

This conversation was one more step toward the development of our Dignity college scholarship program, and the college education of many young women, plus a few men.

Sixty College Graduates
and Counting

I n response to discussions with teachers, principals and
parents, World Dignity established a college scholarship
program for poor students. Sixty students have now
graduated from colleges in Thailand, India, and Bangladesh, with another 25 studying. Only one student has
dropped out. There are at least 60 great stories, but allow
me a few to give you a sense of the students' determination
and of our approach.

****

Our first student lived on a small island off the southern
coast of Thailand. Her family had a very small rubber farm,
which her mom, dad and a brother worked, making at best
a subsistence living. I visited them in their home which was
in great disrepair. Her mom and dad, due to the hard work,
looked much older than their years.

The young woman had been one of the students who
had worked as a tutor in her school, had done well, and

had decided to become a teacher. She was highly recommended by her teachers and principal for college, and we awarded her a scholarship. Part of the agreement she had to sign was that she would return to her village to teach. She has been teaching in the school she attended for about 10 years. She's now a volunteer for our program, vetting and recommending students from the area who apply for Dignity scholarships.

****

Two years ago, a volunteer and I visited one of our Dignity Scholars in southern Thailand to see how he was doing. He had a bad cold that day, but more important to us, he was working two jobs to pay his portion of college expenses and to assist his mother and disabled brother. He was in a computer graphics program, could not afford a computer, having to use a school computer during the night. His grades were understandably suffering.

We had to make a decision. Should we spend more on him? Without more aid, he would likely fail. We deliberated and quickly decided to increase his living expense stipend and to buy him a computer. We thought his hard work and dedication to his family warranted more assistance.

We took him to a computer store and asked him to tell us what he needed. He chose a very inexpensive computer, so we intervened and selected a computer to serve his needs for many years. This was definitely throwing "good money after good money."

Two years later we met with him again to see how he was doing. He was still working his two old jobs plus a third at a computer graphics company, which surprised us. He was doing so well there they offered him a job after his graduation. His mother was deceased and his father was now able to help his disabled son. We were thrilled that his grades were way up and congratulated him on his work at the company. He has matured into a successful student with a promising career.

****

We are impressed with the success of our very first student and the young man's story. Yet, they are only two of the dozens of students World Dignity has seen through college graduation in Thailand, India, and Bangladesh.

We didn't set out to establish a college scholarship program. It grew out of discussions with teachers, principals, and community leaders who told us that many of their high school students could not afford college.

Raising money was only one challenge. Encouraging students, especially girls, to apply for college was not easy, particularly in South India villages where the culture was that girls got married, and stayed at home.

We created a support system for the students once in college, since this would be a difficult experience for them. With the assistance of teachers and principals, we encouraged students with the most potential to apply for college and the scholarships. Then we had volunteers check on the students regularly, requiring them to send us their grades. If they didn't communicate with us and maintain a decent GPA, we could stop giving them funds.

The scholarship programs were tailored to the cultures of India, Thailand, and Bangladesh. For example, the India program provides both grants and loans to the students who must repay the loans for future students support. In Bangladesh, we support only girls who are orphans because they are in the greatest need. And the support system initially developed for Thai students has been modified for India and Bangladesh.

Today, our focus is primarily supporting students in college, using about 80 percent of our funds. Educating one person affects the entire family and the community in perpetuity.

Chapter 12
Reflections on Democracy and Politics

Can There Be Democracy
Where There's No Politics?

In 1651, Thomas Hobbes wrote *Leviathan*, in which he said that life outside society would be "solitary, poor, nasty, brutish, and short." Hobbes thought that every person seeks power over others and would kill for power and food in a world of scarce resources.

I don't believe every single person is the way Hobbes described, but I do believe that without laws, and a way to enforce them, life in that kind of society might well be "solitary, poor, nasty, brutish and short", except for the rapacious few at the top who would have the power and the resources.

Hobbes prescription to avoid the kind of "society" he described was to concentrate power in the king (dictator) who would rule based on truths derived from unquestionable philosophical premises. Thus, a dictator would create a safe society, devoid of controversy, where inhabitants would not live in fear. Some of Hobbes' ideas are still in vogue today.

As was known in Hobbes' day, attempting to eliminate controversy and to create the perfect society through a dictator who knows the "truth" doesn't work. Evolution and different circumstances have led to many different kinds of people who hold a variety of views – "truths" – that must be considered in creating a workable society. Often it's the person with the most outlandish views and way of life to whom we most need to listen.

There's no way to create the perfect society, nor should that be our goal. Our aim should be to create a workable society that allows people, individually and in groups, to learn and grow to their full potential. This cannot happen where one person or the few dominate ideas and ways of organizing society, and where controversy is stifled. It's the essence of politics to reconcile differences and to incorporate as many viewpoints as possible in the laws and regulations of society. That's messy, but that's what politics is all about.

Where dictators rule, and in democracies gone awry, there's little politics. In those societies, controversies are ignored or pushed underground. Laws and rules reflect the ideas of the dictator or a small clique of powerful people. A vibrant democracy stems from a vibrant community, one that reflects the many ideas and interests of most of the people, and where minority views are respected. Where there's no politics, there's no democracy. Where there's no democracy, there's little or no politics.

Is Politics the
Art of the Possible?

Politics as the art of doing the possible could just as well be conceived as the art of doing the impossible. Getting anything complicated done is very difficult and getting something done in the political arena is doubly so. Perhaps politicians should be forgiven if they cannot get much done.

I'm not seeking forgiveness for what I couldn't get done in my 21 years in office, nor am I asking for accolades for what I got done. Besides, not many years after leaving office, most people had forgotten that I led the way for a baseball stadium and a kayak course in downtown South Bend, created a highly diverse city work force, and more.

Although my goals and projects were always important to me, what most absorbed me was the process of reaching those goals and getting projects done. Once projects and goals were on their way to completion, I moved on to other ventures.

My objective in this book was to elucidate my approach to getting things done in the political arena through personal stories detailing how I dealt with projects and incidents, large and small. Through this effort, I hope politicians and the general public may gain insights into political work and their political selves.

Knowing and understanding the intellectual, emotional, and physical demands of effective political work is important for anyone seeking or holding political office who wants to get things done and for the general public. This book is my modest attempt to make you think about these matters.

Twenty-Five Lessons
Learned and Relearned

1. SEEKING POLITICAL OFFICE is a popularity contest, but leadership and governing are not. Planning to get important matters done in politics and wanting to be loved – the occupational hazard of politicians – are mutually exclusive. Important goals generate opposition and lead to the loss of "love" by constituents, even friends.

2. LEADERSHIP AND MANAGEMENT are different. Leadership is articulating a vision, setting long term goals, anticipating challenges, and creating a talented group to meet those goals and challenges. Management is implementing the vision, major goals and decisions made.

3. SERVANT LEADERSHIP doesn't mean simply following popular opinion, it means honesty, educating the public about challenges not fully known or understood, and the courage to do so.

4. FOLLOWING POLLS to figure out what to do is not leadership, it's followership.

5. THE PEOPLE YOU APPOINT make you. Once applicants were deemed technically qualified, here's what I looked for: (1) They've conquered difficulties in their professional and personal lives; (2) Honesty; (3) Not afraid to confront their superior; (4) Enthusiasm for the job and life; (5) Imagination; (6) Someone I'd enjoy working with.

6. I FOCUSED ON STRENGTHS in job applicants, not an absence of weaknesses. Hiring the applicants who have few or no weaknesses ignores the strengths needed in a candidate.

7. THINGS GET DONE by we, not just by I. Although, I used the word I in writing this book and did not name key staff, the accomplishments I described happened with we, not by I.

8. INTELLIGENCE IS OVERRATED. Character is more important. When considering who to vote for, I look for someone who is honest, treats all peoples with respect, listens, and is willing to change.

9. LEARNING AND READING are essential. During my time in government, I read works on management and leadership, and during busy times, I would disappear to Notre Dame to think and to read philosophy, psychology, and theology.

10. "MY WAY OR THE HIGHWAY" often gets in the way of getting something done.

11. PERSISTENCE IN PURSUING an important goal is a virtue; refusing to listen to reason before setting the goal is obstinacy.

12. NOTHING IMPORTANT GETS DONE without opposition, especially in the political arena. If you don't enjoy, or at least tolerate public conflict, don't go into politics.

13. WHAT'S THE WORST that can happen? Prior to making an important decision, or taking a course of action, we always asked ourselves that question and prepared accordingly. As Benjamin Franklin said, "By failing to prepare, you are preparing to fail."

14. "IF YOU'RE DAMNED IF YOU DO and damned if you don't, then do." Whenever I was between a rock and a hard place, which was often, I remembered this saying of Notre Dame's late Rev. Theodore Hesburgh, C.S.C.

15. "VOTE FOR ME, I'M NOT A POLITICIAN." Candidates for political office who say this don't know or understand they're seeking a political position. They say this to get votes because they know that politicians don't enjoy much respect – a dishonest way to begin a political career.

16. ACTIONS SPEAK LOUDER than words, but words speak too. To say words don't lead people to act is being obtuse. Common sense speaks otherwise. Why speak words if they don't have an effect?

17. SATISFY YOUR EGO or improve the community? Both are possible if your goal is to improve the community. My goal was to improve my community and not necessarily to get re-elected. Too many politicians have an eye on the next political job. I learned early to do my job the best I could and let that decide my professional future.

18. CAMPAIGN IN A WAY that will allow you to govern successfully. What's the point of winning if you've done so by

deceiving the public, thus losing their confidence?

19. TRUTH IS THE "MOTHER'S MILK" of politics, not money. Money can help you spread either the truth or deception. The truth will help you lead, while deception will ultimately fail you and the community.

20. DURING A CAMPAIGN for mayor, I told citizens I would raise taxes to provide the excellent services they expected. Some thought this was political suicide. It was not. People appreciated honesty and directness on this issue – at least enough voters did.

21. A LOW TAX CITY is like a low income household. It cannot keep up with essential services and provide for growth.

22. LISTENING TO CITIZENS is important, not only to get a feel for what's on their minds, but for their excellent suggestions on many issues. Many projects such as the downtown kayak course and the baseball stadium were suggested by citizens.

23. "IT IS NOT OUR ABILITIES that show what we truly are. . . it is our choices." From the character "Albus Dumbledore in Harry Potter and the Chamber of Secrets.

24. EVERY PHONE CALL AND LETTER (no email then) was acknowledged within 24 hours. This was my rule prior to politics and still is. It's also being polite which happens to be politically effective.

25. BE YOURSELF. DON'T WORRY what people think of you. Anyway, it's challenging to know yourself deeply and fully – the public is not likely to ever know you either way.

Appendix
Additional Acknowledgements

Remembering Jon R. Hunt

Jon Hunt loved South Bend.
He served her citizens all his adult life
passing away in 2003 after serving 23 years as
Executive Director, Community / Economic Development.

Jon was a quiet and effective leader
who took no credit for his many accomplishments.
He was a critical part of every major neighborhood
and economic development project.
His large vision for South Bend was one
with stronger neighorhoods,
a vibrant downtown, and a strong economy.

No challenge was too great for Jon.
His eternal optimism, dedication,
and hard work kept South Bend moving forward.

Remembering James (Jim) Seitz

Jim Seitz transformed South Bend through his vision
that a city can only be as good as its parks.

His accomplishments during 18 years as Superintendent of
parks are legendary. They include renovating Potawatomi Zoo,
building Boehm and Belleville parks,
and turning an old factory into a hockey rink.

Jim said his most rewarding challenges were
building the Stanley Coveleski stadium (Four Winds Field)
and the East Race kayak course.

Of the two, he most loved the kayak course.
He practically slept there while it was being built.
He had to because it was a one-of-a-kind construction,
testing the talents of the best designers and engineers.

In recognition of Jim's legendary years of service
to South Bend, Mayor Roger Parent named the park
adjacent to the Kayak Course: Seitz Park.

Things Get Done by We, Not Just by I

South Bend Departments and Directors (Alphabetical List)
1980 - 1987

Craig E. Hartzer, Deputy Mayor

Joseph E. Kernan, Controller, Administration & Finance
Michael L. Vance, Controller, Administration & Finance
Katherine G. Barnard, Director,
Code Enforcement Department*
Patricia DeClercq, Director, Code Enforcement Department*
Jon R. Hunt, Director, Community / Economic Development
Timothy Brassell, Chief, Fire Department
Luther T. Taylor, Sr, Chief, Fire Department
Cathy (Hubbard) Grundy-Davis, Director,
Human Resource Department*
Richard Hill, City Attorney, Legal Department
(Corporate Counsel)
Eugenia Schwartz, City Attorney, Legal Department
(Corporate Counsel)
James R. Seitz, Superintendent, Park Department
Michael Borkowski, Chief, Police Department
Dan Thompson, Chief, Police Department
Charles T. Hurley, Chief, Police Department
Patrick McMahon, Director, Public Works Department
John E. Leszczynski, Director, Public Works Department
Robert Goodrich, Director, Recreation Department

* New Departments
**Apologies to those I may have missed.

1987 Park Board and Redevelopment Commissioners

Redevelopment Commissioners

F. Jay Nimtz
Paula N. Auburn
Sandy Combs
Michael Donoho
Roman J. Piasecki

Jon Hunt, Executive Director

Park Board Members

Richard J. Kromkowski
Gwendolyne E. Stiver
Melvin L Holmes
John L. Horvath

James R. Seitz, Superintendent

City Clerk and City Council Members, 1980-1987

Irene Gammon, City Clerk

Joseph T. Serge, 1st District
Walter M. Szymkowiak, 2nd District
Eugenia Braboy, 2nd District
Beverlie Beck, 3rd District
Lewis A. McGann, 4th District
Ann B. Puzzello, 4th District
Robert G. Taylor, 5th District
Walter Kopczynski, 6th District
Raymond C. Zelinski, 6th District
Thomas Zakrewski, 6th District

James Barcome, At l arge
Beverly D. Crone, At large
Richard Dombrowski, At large
John J. Harris, Jr., At large
Al B. Paszek, At large
John Voorde, At large

*Note some resignations and others losing in 1983
elections accounts for more than one person in the position.*

Roger Parent Biography

Elected Positions

Mayor, South Bend, Indiana, 8 years, 1980-1987
City Council, South Bend, 8 years,
    President, 5 years, 1972-1979
School Board Member, South Bend, 5 ½ years,
    President, 2 years, 2009-2014

Other Leadership Positions

President, RIPEA (Retired Indiana Public Employee
    Association) Current
President and Founder, World Dignity, Inc.
    (Non-profit) Current
Peace Corps Country Director, Haiti, Grenada, 1988-1990,
    and Bulgaria later.
Peace Corps Volunteer, First Thailand Group, 1961-63

Publications and Teaching

Parent, Roger, *The Making of a Peace Corps Volunteer: From
    Maine to Thailand*, Published, 2013, 200 pages.
Parent, Roger, "La Petite Boucanne Bleu" ECHOES:
    Rediscovering Community, The Northern Maine Journal of
    Rural Culture, No. 39, Jan. - March, 1998. (Plus a dozen
    more articles in this magazine.)
Parent, Roger, Book Review in DIMENSIONS, July/Aug,
    1998, NCDC. Kelly, Kathleen S.,
Effective Fund-Raising Management, 1998.
Parent, Roger, *Amelia Discovers the Secret of Her Dove*,
    unpublished young adult novel, 2015
Adjunct Lecturer, 1990 ~ 1993: Indiana University and
    Indiana/Purdue Universities. (Courses: Decision-Making
    and Policy-Making in Government)

continued

Other Credentials

B.A. Degree in Economics, Magna Cum Laude, May 1961, St. Francis Xavier University, Antigonish, Nova Scotia, Canada. M.A. Degree in Education, May, 1966, University of Notre Dame, Indiana. Languages: Fluent in French and English. Spoken Thai.

Married to Rolande Ouellette Parent. We have four children and six grandchildren.